WHEN IT COMES TO LIFE

WHEN IT COMES TO LIFE

127 Effective Lessons, Principles,
and Considerations for Daily Living

C.M. PROCTOR

COPYRIGHT © 2024 C. M. PROCTOR
All rights reserved.

WHEN IT COMES TO LIFE
127 Effective Lessons, Principles, and Considerations for Daily Living

FIRST EDITION

ISBN   978-1-5445-4507-3 *Hardcover*
           978-1-5445-4508-0 *Paperback*
           978-1-5445-4509-7 *Ebook*

To my family and friends, past, present, and future—for their unwavering support and guidance. Thank you for teaching me valuable lessons, both directly and indirectly, and for giving me the freedom to make mistakes and create successes. Your love and support have been instrumental in shaping who I am today. I am grateful for your presence in my life and cherish the lessons we have learned together.

CONTENTS

INTRODUCTION 9

PERSONAL INDEX 15

I. DISCIPLINE, RESILIENCE, AND PRODUCTIVITY 17

II. TEAMWORK, RELATIONSHIPS 77

III. PERSONAL DEVELOPMENT 103

IV. PROBLEM-SOLVING 175

V. COMMUNICATION AND INTERPERSONAL SKILLS 193

VI. PERSONAL RESPONSIBILITY 227

VII. CONCLUSION 263

ACKNOWLEDGEMENTS 267

REFERENCES 269

INTRODUCTION

"I cannot teach anybody anything. I can only make them think."
—SOCRATES

WHEN IT COMES TO LIFE, WE ASK MANY QUESTIONS ABOUT who we want to be and what we want to achieve. *What are my values, my passions, my unique talents and abilities?* Discovering the answers to these questions is a crucial step in building a fulfilling and purposeful existence. Every one of us has the potential to become a strong and influential individual, but this kind of growth and development requires a deep understanding of ourselves and our goals.

When we feel lost in these questions, we look to the strong influences in our lives for counsel. It is easy to assume our heroes were simply born with some kind of gift or had a wise mentor guiding them along their way. However, many of these individuals achieved their success through hard work, determination, and a relentless pursuit of their goals. Those people asked themselves the same questions we must ask ourselves:

Who do I want to be? What do I want to be known for? How do I want people to see me? Then, they set out to create a plan to achieve their vision. The unifying feature of these influential figures is that they were lifelong learners.

Passion for learning and self-improvement should be a driving force in your life. As soon as you have any control, you should be committed to excellence in every field you enter and constantly seeking to expand your knowledge and skills. Curiosity and hunger for knowledge should extend to—and far beyond—the horizons of our experiences. These traits are essential so that you, too, can become a strong influence in the lives of others and a model for a life of virtue and learning.

This book is a companion guide for your self-reflection as you clear your own unique path through life. As you explore these pages, I am excited to share with you a wealth of hard-earned insights and practical wisdom I have gathered from my personal and professional experiences as a fellow traveller on the path of self-improvement.

From discipline, resilience, and productivity to teamwork, relationships, personal development, problem-solving, communication, and personal responsibility, I have sought to cover a wide range of topics essential for success in today's fast-paced and challenging world.

As an individual constantly striving for self-improvement and growth, I have dedicated my life to learning, observing, and extracting valuable lessons from my successes and failures. During my downtime, I have avidly delved into numerous books, audiobooks, podcasts, and courses to broaden my perspectives and enhance my abilities in various domains. Through my extensive self-learning and development efforts, I have gained diverse insights and experiences that have shaped my perspectives on life and provided me with valuable lessons and considerations for navigating its challenges and opportunities. I do not claim to have all the answers, but I have demonstrated my commitment, faced challenges head-on, and learned valuable lessons along the way. It is my honour to share these lessons with you, the reader, in the hope that they will empower you to navigate the complexities of life with resilience, discipline, and purpose.

Each of the 127 lessons, considerations, and words of advice presented in this book provides actionable steps intended to empower you, the reader, with practical tools and insights that you can apply in your daily life to support your personal development.

The key to becoming a strong and influential individual lies in your ability to take ownership of our own growth. It is important to recognize that this kind of growth and development is not a one-time event but an ongoing process. As we move through life, our goals and priorities may change, and we must be willing to adapt and evolve. This means continuing to ask ourselves important questions and be willing to make changes and adjustments as needed. By creating a vision for our lives and taking consistent action toward our goals, we can become the best versions of ourselves and leave a lasting impact on the world.

Success in any area of your life requires commitment and effort. No matter what goal you set for yourself, putting in even the slightest amount of work each day will help you achieve that goal over time. This is true whether you're striving to excel in your chosen career, build stronger relationships, or develop new skills and abilities. But achieving your goals isn't just about excelling in one area of your life. It's also about maintaining balance and giving proper attention to all the important aspects of your life. Different areas may require different levels of focus at different times, but it's critical that no key area is neglected, lest you throw off the balance you've worked so hard to achieve. The path of life is often one of uncertainty and unpredictability, and for many people, it can be tempting to simply wait and see what happens.

However, you were drawn to this book because you are not content with an average life and seek further improvement. Whether you are actively pursuing change or simply open to new ideas and concepts, the content within these pages is intended to challenge your thinking and help you understand the forces that drive your life and decisions. By exploring new ideas and concepts, you will gain a deeper understanding of yourself and your values, and you will be better equipped to make the changes you desire.

For each lesson and consideration in the coming chapters, you'll find the lesson name, descriptive categories, explanation of the lesson/consideration, and action steps you can practise in your day-to-day life. Some action steps may be repetitive and apply to multiple lessons, but they are intentionally included to stress the importance of consistent and deliberate practise. View each lesson individually, with its own action steps, or as part of the whole. Remember: true change comes from consistent action, not just reading and learning.

Use the Personal Index that follows to record the fifteen most impactful lessons for you, along with their page numbers for easy future reference. Interpretations of these lessons may change, and those fifteen might not always be your "most impactful." They may even become ingrained into your daily way of thinking so that when these are reflected upon later in life, you almost wonder what made them stand out so much at the time of reading. That is the growth that I've experienced during my journey of knowledge, and I hope to have the same take place in your life as well.

I am deeply grateful for the opportunity to share my insights and experiences with you in this book. I sincerely believe that the knowledge and wisdom presented within these pages will resonate with you and empower you to lead a more fulfilling and purpose-driven life. By reflecting on these timeless insights and implementing them in your daily life, you can make positive changes that will help you achieve your goals. Most of all, I hope you enjoy reading this collection of lessons as much as I enjoyed writing it.

PERSONAL INDEX

"The things you think about determine the quality of your mind. Your soul takes on the colour of your thoughts."

—MARCUS AURELIUS, *MEDITATIONS*

USE THIS PERSONAL INDEX TO HIGHLIGHT YOUR CHOSEN fifteen lessons of impact and write the page number in the box on the right for quick reference.

LESSON	PAGE NO.

DISCIPLINE, RESILIENCE, AND PRODUCTIVITY

"Progress is not achieved by luck or accident, but by working on yourself daily."

—EPICTETUS

WELCOME TO THE WORLD OF PERSONAL GROWTH AND self-improvement. Life can be challenging and demanding, and navigating through its ups and downs requires discipline, resilience, and productivity. This chapter will explore these three crucial themes and how they relate to unlocking success in all aspects of your life.

Discipline is the foundation on which success is built. It's about self-control and determination to stay focused on your goals, even when faced with distractions, obstacles, and temptations. Discipline enables you to make tough choices, prioritize your time and resources, and consistently take action toward your desired outcomes. By mastering discipline, readers will learn how to overcome procrastination, develop healthy habits, and cultivate a mindset of perseverance and commitment.

Resilience is the key to bouncing back from setbacks and challenges. Life is full of obstacles and failures, and how we respond to them determines our success. Resilience is about developing mental toughness, emotional strength, and adaptability to face adversity head-on and come out stronger on the other side. By cultivating resilience, you will learn how to handle stress, overcome failures, and maintain a positive attitude in the face of challenges.

Productivity is the art of optimizing your time, energy, and resources to achieve your goals efficiently and effectively. It's about managing your tasks, setting priorities, and maximizing your output to achieve the desired results. Productivity is not about working harder but working smarter. By mastering productivity, you will learn how to optimize workflow, set meaningful goals, and achieve greater efficiency in daily life.

As we dive into the lessons in this chapter, I will provide you with actionable steps to implement discipline, resilience, and productivity in your life. I will then guide you on how to apply these themes to your unique situations and unlock success in all aspects of your life through practical tips, real-life examples, and exercises. Change can be challenging, and implementing new habits and mindset shifts may not be easy. However, the rewards of discipline, resilience, and productivity are worth the effort. By mastering these essential life skills, you will be equipped with the tools and mindset necessary to overcome challenges, achieve goals, and thrive in your personal and professional endeavours.

In the following lessons, we will explore the principles,

strategies, and practical steps to develop discipline, resilience, and productivity in your life. Whether you want to improve your career, relationships, health, or personal development, these lessons will provide valuable insights and actionable steps to unlock your full potential. So, let's dive in and discover how discipline, resilience, and productivity can improve your life. The journey begins.

DO ALL THINGS WELL

Designation: Discipline, Attention to Detail, Leadership

LESSON:

Do things well, whether you think they're worth your time or not. Do them with purpose and conviction. Aim to do even the most minuscule task assigned to you or that comes across your path in the very best way you can. It will set a standard for yourself and those around you, especially if they are tasks that you, as a leader, could have left to someone in a position below yours but chose not to. How you approach each task in your life sets a standard for yourself and those around you. When we do something, we should give it our all and do it with purpose and conviction. It doesn't matter if it's a task you believe is beneath your capabilities or one that seems menial; every action we take sets a precedent for the people around us.

In a leadership capacity, it is not just about making decisions and delegating tasks. It's also about setting an example and leading by action. When we take the time to do things well, no matter how small they may seem, we demonstrate the importance of doing those things to the best of our abilities to those around us. This contagious mindset can inspire others to put in effort also and give their all in every task they undertake. This approach to work demonstrates a level of personal responsibility and dedication not often seen in today's society. It showcases a commitment to excellence, respect for the work itself, and respect for those who entrust it to you. This kind of work ethic has a ripple effect, inspiring those around you to do the same: put in the extra effort and strive for excellence in their own work. The result is a collective effort of purpose, a shared vision of success, and a team working together to achieve it. By doing things well, regardless of perceived worth, you set a standard for yourself and those around you based on the principles of hard work, dedication, and the pursuit of excellence.

ACTION STEPS:

- *Take pride in your work:* Understand that your work is a reflection of yourself. By taking pride in your work, you show respect for yourself, your colleagues, and the work itself.
- *Focus on the process:* Break down the task or project into smaller, more manageable steps, and focus on doing each step to the best of your ability. This can help you stay engaged and motivated and create a sense of momentum and progress as you move toward the final outcome.
- *Set clear standards and expectations:* Identify what you want to achieve and define what "well" means to you in the context of the task or project. This can help you stay focused and motivated and create a clear sense of direction as you work toward your goal.
- *Seek feedback and learn from mistakes:* Ask others for input and advice, and be open to constructive criticism and suggestions for improvement. When things don't go as planned,

take the time to reflect on what happened and identify what you can do differently in the future. This can help you grow and develop as you work toward doing things even better in the future.

COURSE ADJUSTMENTS—AN ANALOGY

Designation: Discipline, Resilience, Goal Setting

LESSON:

Picture a rocket heading toward your target, the moon. You program the coordinates, and the rocket begins its lengthy ascent. As it gets closer, however, you realize it is off course, and you should have made slight adjustments throughout the rocket's journey. Just like a rocket, our lives have a trajectory, and every decision you make has the potential to alter that trajectory. This analogy is an excellent illustration of the importance of staying focused on our path. A couple degrees off course may seem insignificant, but it can significantly impact the final destination. The same can be said for our lives. Slight deviations from our path can add up over time, leading us further away from our goals and desires.

To stay on course, the rocket must constantly make adjustments, correcting its trajectory and realigning with its target. In the same way, we must also stay focused and disciplined in our pursuit of goals and dreams. It's all too easy to get distracted or sidetracked, but it's essential to remember that every decision we make can impact our trajectory. We must remain vigilant and intentional about our choices, ensuring they align with our goals and values.

Staying focused also requires us to be proactive and take

charge of our lives. Instead of simply responding to the world around us, we must take the reins and actively shape our trajectory. This requires a clear vision of where we want to go and the determination to make it happen.

A clear vision is also necessary if your goal is to make it as far as possible in life. You don't want to shoot for the moon and land there if it isn't your desired target. A few small changes here and there can change our trajectory; with focus, discipline, and proactive choices, we can stay on course and reach our destination.

ACTION STEPS:

- *Reflect regularly:* Take time regularly to reflect on your current situation and assess whether you are on track to achieve your goals. This could be as simple as spending fifteen minutes at the end of each day to review your accomplishments and areas where you could improve.
- *Set small, achievable goals:* Instead of making big changes all at once, break your goals down into smaller, more manageable steps. This will make it easier to adjust your course as needed and to celebrate small wins along the way.
- *Be flexible:* Life is unpredictable, and it's important to adapt to changing circumstances. When things don't go as planned, try to stay open-minded and look for new opportunities to learn and grow. Remember, setbacks are not failures; they are simply opportunities to course-correct and try again.

DAYS YOU DON'T FEEL LIKE IT

Designation: Discipline, Perseverance

LESSON:

Days where we don't feel our best can be difficult to navigate, but they also represent a unique life challenge. Far too many people accept these days as excuses to simply coast through. But to truly make the most of our lives, we must approach difficult days with a different mindset. By pushing ourselves to be as productive—or even more so—on these days, we demonstrate to ourselves and the world that we are not limited by our circumstances. It's easy to be caught up in the idea that life will always be easy and we will always feel our best, but that is far from the truth. Life will throw us curveballs, but how we handle these difficulties truly defines who we are. When we push ourselves to be productive on days when we don't feel our best, we show the world and ourselves that our circumstances do not define us.

We also demonstrate our resilience, fortitude, and determination by embracing these challenges and pushing through. These qualities help us navigate life's difficulties, and they are developed through pushing ourselves in challenging situations. We may not always feel like pushing ourselves on these days, but because of this discomfort, we grow and become stronger. It's not always easy, but by embracing these challenges, we can transform them into opportunities for growth and self-discovery.

ACTION STEPS:

- *Create a routine:* Creating a routine can help you maintain momentum on days when you don't feel like it. Even if you don't feel motivated, having a set routine can help you stay on track and maintain a sense of structure. This could involve creating a schedule for your day or setting aside specific times for work or exercise.
- *Find inspiration:* Finding sources of inspiration can help you stay motivated on days when you don't feel like it. This could involve seeking inspirational quotes or stories, listening to music or podcasts that inspire you, or spending time in nature. Whatever motivates you, make sure to incorporate it into your routine and use it as a source of energy when you're feeling unmotivated.
- *Set realistic expectations:* If all else fails, be realistic about your abilities and what you can achieve on days you don't feel like acting on your priorities. Don't set yourself up for failure by expecting to be highly productive when feeling unmotivated. Instead, focus on small, achievable goals that will help you progress, even if it's just a little bit.

DOUBLING DOWN DURING TIMES OF PROGRESS

Designation: Discipline

LESSON:

If you've been doing something that works in a way where you start to see progress, this is the opposite of the time to let up. Double down on your efforts and continue on the path. Seeing progress highlights the importance of persistence and discipline in achieving success. When we have found a method that yields results, it is essential to maintain focus and not become complacent. Instead, we should strive to increase our efforts and work even harder to continue making progress. Whether faced with challenges or temptations to give up, we must remain dedicated and committed to our goals. By doing so, we increase the likelihood of continued success and growth. By doubling down on our efforts and staying the course, we increase the odds of reaching our desired outcomes and making our dreams a reality.

This also stresses the importance of avoiding distractions and temptations that may cause us to veer off course. By continuing to work diligently and making progress, we build momentum and create a positive cycle of growth and success. On the other hand, giving up or becoming complacent after seeing initial progress can be detrimental, leading to stagnation and the loss of progress. It is important to understand that success is not a destination but a journey that requires constant effort and dedication. Therefore, it is crucial to maintain a steadfast focus and not let up when we start to see progress. This requires discipline, self-control, and determination, but the rewards of continued growth and success make it worthwhile.

ACTION STEPS:

- *Identify what's working and why:* Take the time to analyze the factors that contributed to your progress, such as your team's strengths, your decision-making process, or your resources. Identify the key drivers of success so you can continue to build on them.
- *Double down on your efforts:* It can be tempting to slow down or become complacent when you are making progress. However, it's vital to double down on your efforts and push

forward. This can involve setting ambitious goals, investing in new resources, or taking on new challenges. By doubling down on your efforts, you can accelerate your progress and create even more momentum for future success.

- *Celebrate your progress:* Celebrate your progress and your team's progress. Take the time to recognize your achievements and milestones. Celebrate your successes in a way that's meaningful to you and your team, whether with a team outing, a special meal, or a simple recognition ceremony. This can help build momentum and motivation for future progress.

CREATING STRUCTURE, EVEN AMONG CHAOS

Designation: Discipline, Resilience, Leadership

LESSON:

Creating structure, even among chaos, is a crucial leadership skill that separates the best leaders from the rest. In any situation—but especially in chaotic ones—having a clear plan of action and a defined structure to back you up can help bring order and calm. As a leader, it's essential to understand that chaos is a natural part of life. But how you respond to that chaos makes all the difference. Creating a structured approach can turn a chaotic situation into an opportunity to shine. To do this, take a step back and assess the situation. This will allow you to identify the key elements of the chaos and prioritize the necessary actions to bring order. Once you have a clear understanding of what needs to be done, you can begin to create a plan of action. Your plan should include clear goals, defined responsibilities, and a timeline for completion. Communicate this plan to your team and ensure everyone understands their role in bringing order to the chaos. But it's not enough to create a plan and hope for the best. You must also adjust and adapt your plan as needed. This means staying flexible and open to new ideas and being willing to make changes when necessary.

The same applies to nonleadership roles. Once you break down a situation or set of tasks and create that structure, you can develop your independence or leadership skills, build trust with those around you, and lead all involved to success. So take charge, assess the situation, and create a plan of action that will bring order to the chaos and lead you to victory in the goals you set out to complete.

ACTION STEPS:

- *Create a process:* Amid chaos, creating a structured process for completing tasks can be helpful. This can involve breaking down large tasks into smaller, more manageable steps and creating a checklist to help you stay on track. Creating a process can create a sense of order and direction and prevent important tasks from falling through the cracks.
- *Communicate and collaborate:* When chaos strikes, it's important to communicate with others and work collaboratively to create structure. This can involve delegating tasks to others, seeking input and feedback from colleagues, and establishing clear lines of communication. By working together, you can create a more efficient and effective process for completing tasks and creating structure, even during chaos.
- *Prioritize and organize:* When faced with chaos, it can be overwhelming to know where to start. To create structure, start by prioritizing your tasks and organizing your time.

Determine the most urgent and important tasks, and create a plan to tackle them first. This can help you regain control and focus and prevent you from getting bogged down by less important tasks.

PUT YOURSELF NEXT IN LINE

Designation: Discipline, Self-Advocacy, Taking Initiative

LESSON:

If you don't put yourself next in line, how do you expect to be chosen? This statement highlights the importance of taking initiative and putting yourself in a position to be recognized and selected for opportunities. In life, many people wait for opportunities to come, hoping that someone will notice their potential and offer them a chance to grow and succeed. However, this approach is not always practical, as prospects do not simply fall into our laps. If you want to be chosen for opportunities, you must put yourself next in line. This means actively seeking the opportunities that align with your goals and aspirations and demonstrating your value and worth to those who have the power to choose. You must put yourself in a position where you can be seen and heard and showcase your skills and talents to the main decision-makers in the roles you seek.

One way to do this is to network and build relationships with people in your industry or field. When you connect with others who share your interests and goals, you can learn about new opportunities and position yourself to be considered for them. Additionally, when you build strong relationships with others, they are more likely to recommend you for positions and opportunities that they know will be suitable for you.

Another way is to continually improve and develop your skills and knowledge. You increase your value and worth by continuously learning and growing, making yourself a more attractive candidate. Whether taking courses, reading books, or seeking mentorship, investing in your personal and professional development will help you stand out from the crowd.

Don't wait for opportunities to come to you; go out and create them. If you have a passion or idea, take the initiative to pursue it and make it a reality. This shows initiative and demonstrates your ability to take control of your life and future. By putting yourself in a position where you can be seen and heard and continuously improving and growing, you increase your chances of being chosen for the opportunities you desire.

ACTION STEPS:
- *Build relationships:* One of the most effective ways to put yourself next in line for opportunities is to build strong relationships with people in your industry or field of interest. Attend industry events, join professional organizations, and network with other professionals. By building relationships, you'll be more likely to hear about upcoming opportunities and be top of mind when someone is looking for a candidate.
- *Develop your skills:* Another important step to put yourself next in line for opportunities is to develop your skills and expertise. Look for ways to learn and grow, such as taking courses, attending workshops or conferences, or volunteering for projects. By continually developing your skills, you'll be better equipped to take advantage of opportunities.
- *Be proactive:* To put yourself next in line for opportunities, you need to be proactive. Don't wait for opportunities to come to you—seek them out. Keep an eye on job boards,

industry publications, and social media to stay current on upcoming opportunities. And when you see an opportunity that interests you, don't hesitate to reach out and express your interest. Being proactive will make you stand out for any opportunity that arises.

CHOOSING BATTLES WISELY

Designation: Prioritization, Decision-Making, Leadership

LESSON:

Choosing your battles wisely is a key aspect of an effective life. It is important to weigh the potential outcomes of a conflict before engaging. Many situations can be resolved with a calm, rational conversation, but sometimes, pursuing a resolution is not worth the time or energy. Knowing when to step back and focus your efforts on more pressing matters is crucial. When faced with conflict, it is important to consider whether it is a "life or death" situation. If it isn't, think carefully about the potential consequences of speaking out. Many risks are involved in confronting someone, but there can also be great rewards. For example, you may gain respect and earn trust by standing up for yourself or others. On the other hand, if the situation is not worth the potential consequences, it may be best to simply walk away and focus your energy on more important battles.

Ultimately, it is up to you to determine which battles are necessary for your growth. Life is full of risks and rewards, and it is essential to choose wisely. Whether it's a conflict with a superior, a disagreement with a friend, or a decision about where to invest your time and energy, weighing the potential outcomes and making informed decisions is important. By doing so, you will be better prepared to face the challenges and opportunities that come your way.

ACTION STEPS:

- *Identify your values and priorities:* Before engaging in any battle or conflict, it's important to first identify your values and priorities. What matters most to you? What are your long-term goals? Understanding your values and priorities can help you determine which battles are worth fighting and which are not worth the time, energy, or emotional investment.
- *Assess the situation:* Consider the potential risks and rewards of engaging in the conflict. Is it something that can be resolved through communication and compromise? Is it a battle that will help you achieve your goals, or is it simply a distraction? Be realistic about the potential outcomes of the battle, and consider whether the benefits outweigh the costs.
- *Practise emotional regulation:* Choosing your battles wisely also requires emotional regulation. When you feel provoked or challenged, take a step back and assess the situation objectively. Practise deep breathing or mindfulness techniques to help you remain calm and focused. Pausing your emotions can help you make more rational and thoughtful decisions and avoid getting drawn into battles that are not worth fighting. Remember, sometimes the most powerful response is to choose not to engage.

"WE DON'T RISE TO THE LEVEL OF OUR EXPECTATIONS, WE FALL TO THE LEVEL OF OUR TRAINING."
—ARCHILOCHUS

Designation: Discipline, Preparation

LESSON:

This quote highlights the importance of preparation and training in achieving success, emphasizing that we don't simply rise to the level of our expectations, but rather, we are limited by the level of our preparation and training. Archilochus underscores the need for consistent and deliberate effort in developing the skills and knowledge necessary to reach our goals. Whether striving for success in our personal or professional lives, we must devote hard work and dedication. We must be willing to invest the time and effort to develop the skills, knowledge, and habits necessary to reach our desired outcomes.

Archilochus's words also remind us that our expectations are only as high as the level of preparation we put into achieving them. If we have high aspirations but do not put in the necessary effort to back them up, we are setting ourselves up for disappointment. On the other hand, if we are prepared and put in work, we are much more likely to succeed. This wisdom is a powerful reminder of the importance of preparation and training in reaching our goals. It highlights the need for consistent effort and the value of investing time and energy into developing the necessary skills and knowledge for success.

In the words of Jordan B. Peterson, "Expectations are nothing but hopes and dreams, whereas training is the concrete manifestation of those expectations through effort and discipline." This means we cannot simply hope for success and expect it to come. Instead, we must actively prepare and train for it. Training and preparation are crucial in all areas of life, whether it be personal development, career advancement, or relationships. We will inevitably fall short of our expectations and goals without proper preparation and training. However, with consistent and focused training, we can elevate our abilities and reach new levels of success. This requires discipline, determination, and a willingness to constantly learn and grow. It is a lifelong process that is well worth the effort. The words of Archilochus remind us of the importance of preparation and training in achieving success. By putting in the effort and discipline necessary to reach our goals, we can rise above our expectations and reach new heights.

ACTION STEPS:
- *Develop good habits:* The foundation of good training is developing good habits. Identify the habits that will support the achievement of your goals, and create a plan to implement and reinforce those habits in your daily life. For example, if you want to improve your fitness, establish a regular exercise routine and commit to it, even on days when you don't feel motivated. Consider the skills you can do on autopilot: those are what you fall into at the level of your training.
- *Practise deliberate practise:* Deliberate practise is a technique experts in various fields use to continually improve their skills. It involves breaking down complex skills into manageable pieces and practising those pieces until they become automatic. This can help you develop competence and confidence in your abilities and prepare you for unexpected challenges.
- *Continuously learn and adapt:* To maintain a high per-

formance level, it's important to continuously learn and adapt. Seek new challenges and experiences, and be open to feedback and critique. Evaluation can help you identify improvement areas and develop new skills and techniques to address them. By continuously learning and adapting, you can stay ahead of the curve and remain at the top of your game.

DON'T JUST "DO THE JOB YOU'RE PAID FOR"

Designation: Discipline, Limiting Beliefs

LESSON:

It is a common refrain that some individuals believe they are not being compensated or recognized appropriately for their skills and talents within the workplace. But instead of being discouraged, these individuals should take a proactive approach and strive to go above and beyond in their work to show their value to their employer. Doing so can lead to being recognized and promoted within the organization, or it may lead to realizing that it's time to find a new place of employment where your talents can be properly acknowledged. The key is never settling for mediocrity and pushing yourself to reach your full potential. Whether in the workplace or life, putting in effort and hard work can lead to remarkable outcomes and personal growth. It's important to note that taking the initiative and putting in extra effort can be a key factor in growth. However, it's also important to have realistic expectations and not be discouraged if you do not achieve your desired outcome. In such a scenario, reassessing the situation and seeking opportunities that align with your skills and values may lead to better results. Ultimately, it is up to each individual to take control of their own career path and not simply settle for what is handed to them. It takes determination, hard work, and perseverance to succeed, but the reward of personal fulfilment and growth is worth the effort.

Another aspect to consider is that by putting in the extra effort and doing more than is required, you are also setting yourself apart and demonstrating your commitment to the company and your role. This can lead to increased recognition and rewards and open up new opportunities for growth and development within the organization. Taking initiative and striving for excellence in your work can also improve your skills and abilities, making you a valuable asset to any organization. However, remember that not every employer may value or recognize these efforts. In such cases, it is important to assess whether it is time to move on to a new opportunity where your talents and contributions will be appreciated. Ultimately, the choice is yours, but by continuously striving to improve and do your best, you are making a statement about your value and worth.

ACTION STEPS:

- *Take initiative:* Taking initiative is an important way to go above and beyond your job duties. Look for opportunities to improve processes or solve problems, even if they fall outside of your job description. By taking ownership of your work and looking for ways to add value, you can show your employer that you are committed to your job and interested in the success of the company.
- *Learn new skills:* This is another way to go above and beyond in your job. Look for opportunities to attend training ses-

sions or conferences, or seek mentors who can help you develop new skills. By constantly expanding your knowledge and skillset, you can become a more valuable employee and potentially qualify for new opportunities within the company.

- *Build relationships:* Building relationships within your company is another way to add value beyond your job duties. Get to know your colleagues and superiors, and look for ways to collaborate with them on projects or initiatives. By building a strong network within your company, you can create opportunities for yourself and potentially advance in your career.
- *Volunteer for additional responsibilities:* Don't be afraid to volunteer for additional responsibilities that may not be part of your job description. This can help you gain new experiences and skills and show your employer that you are willing to go above and beyond to contribute to the success of the company.

DO NOT SEEK RECOGNITION

Designation: Discipline, Humility, Selflessness

LESSON:

Do not seek recognition. Consistently work on your craft to better yourself, and recognition will come. When you focus on constantly improving your skills and becoming the best version of yourself, recognition will come naturally. Working on your craft requires dedication, commitment, and a willingness to learn and grow. It involves taking the time to hone your skills, develop new ones, and always strive for self-improvement. Whether it is through reading books, attending workshops, or seeking mentorship and guidance, it is important to put in the effort to continuously improve your skills and knowledge. By focusing on your own personal growth and development, you will not only become a better person, but you will also become more attractive to others. People are drawn to those who are confident and competent, and who have a strong sense of purpose and direction. And when you have a reputation for being knowledgeable, skillful, and dedicated, recognition will come naturally.

Keep in mind that recognition should never be the ultimate goal. Instead, focus on the process of becoming the best version of yourself and let recognition be a by-product of your hard work and dedication. When you focus on improving yourself, you can enjoy the satisfaction of personal growth, and you will find that recognition will come to you when the time is right.

ACTION STEPS:
- *Focus on the work, not the credit:* When working on a project, focus on doing the best job you can, rather than seeking recognition or credit. Take pride in the quality of your work, and seek feedback and guidance from others to help you improve. This will help you develop a reputation as a hard worker and someone who takes pride in their work, which can lead to recognition and respect over time.
- *Collaborate with others:* Working collaboratively with others can help you focus on the task at hand rather than seeking recognition for yourself. By working with others, you can leverage each other's strengths and build a stronger, more effective team. Additionally, when a team is successful, recognition often follows for all members rather than just one individual.

- *Recognize the contributions of others:* A key to not seeking recognition is recognizing the contributions of others. When someone on your team does good work, acknowledge it and give credit where it's due. Doing so creates a positive team dynamic and builds a culture of mutual support and respect. This can also help to create a sense of ownership and investment in the team's success, which can ultimately lead to greater recognition for the team as a whole.

TRY NOT TO STRESS OVER THINGS OUTSIDE YOUR CONTROL

Designation: Mindset, Mental Health

LESSON:

Try not to stress over things outside your control. Stress and anxiety are natural human emotions that can be triggered by many different events and situations. However, it is important to understand that not all stress is created equal. Some stress is a necessary and healthy response to challenges, while other stress is a waste of time and energy. The key to managing stress is to focus on what you can control and let go of what you can't. It is easy to get caught up in worry and stress over things outside of your control. This type of stress is often unproductive and can even harm your health and well-being. The best way to deal with this type of stress is to assess the situation, break it into smaller, more manageable parts, and focus on what you *can* control.

One of the most effective ways to reduce stress is to identify the controllable factors in a situation. Ask yourself questions like: "What can I do right now?" "What needs to wait?" "What do I have no control over?" By breaking down the situation into smaller parts, you can better understand what you can control and what you can't, and you can focus your energy and efforts on the parts that matter most. Another important factor in reducing stress is to have a plan. It's easy to become overwhelmed when looking at a situation from a broad point of view. However, by breaking circumstances down into smaller parts and creating a plan, you can avoid feeling overwhelmed and be better prepared to handle any issues that may arise. This process can also help you identify potential risks and develop strategies to mitigate them. By taking these steps, you can better manage stress and avoid feeling overwhelmed by situations outside your control.

ACTION STEPS:

- *Practise mindfulness:* Mindfulness is being present and aware of the current moment without judgment. It can help you focus on the present and not get caught up in worries about the future or regrets about the past. You can practise mindfulness through meditation, breathing exercises, or simply focusing on the present moment.
- *Take action where you can:* Even if you cannot control the outcome of a situation, you can still take action where possible. Identify the actions you can take to influence conditions and focus on those actions. Doing so can make you feel more empowered and less stressed about things outside of your control.
- *Reframe your thinking:* When you find yourself stressing about something, try to reframe your thinking. Instead of focusing on what you cannot control, focus on what you can control. Accept that some things are outside your capacity, and focus your energy on the things you can influence.

THE BEST YOU CAN DO IS YOUR BEST

Designation: Self-Acceptance, Self-Compassion

LESSON:

The best you can do is your best. Life is unpredictable, and it's not always possible to control the outcome of our efforts. However, what we can manage is the effort we put in and the attitude we have toward our failures. It's essential to remember that as long as we have given it our best, there's nothing more we could have done. If we have exhausted all our abilities and resources and haven't achieved the desired result, then it might be time to let it go and move on. Many people fear failure and think it's a reflection of their inadequacies or shortcomings. However, that's not always the case. Failure is a part of life, and we learn and grow through our failures. The important thing is to keep trying and never give up on our dreams and aspirations. Even if we fail, people will still see us trying and appreciate our efforts.

It's important to realize that sometimes our failures can turn out to be blessings in disguise. They may lead us down a path we never considered, or they may teach us valuable lessons we wouldn't have otherwise learned. So, even if we don't succeed in our endeavours, we should take it as an opportunity to learn and grow as individuals. We should not fear failure, but instead embrace it. Our failures may not define us, but our attitude toward them certainly does. If we have the courage to keep trying, others will nonetheless appreciate our efforts.

ACTION STEPS:

- *Set realistic and achievable goals:* The first step to doing your best is to set realistic and achievable goals. This will help you stay focused and motivated, and avoid feeling overwhelmed or discouraged.
- *Prioritize and manage your time effectively:* To do your best, you need to prioritize your tasks and manage your time effectively. This means identifying what is important and urgent, and allocating your time accordingly.
- *Learn from your mistakes and failures:* Remember that doing your best does not mean being perfect. Mistakes and failures are opportunities to learn and grow. Embrace blunders as part of the process, and use them to improve your skills and performance and, over time, to become better.

CONTINUOUS LEARNING

Designation: Curiosity, Learning

LESSON:

Your thirst for knowledge should always be unquenched. Always strive to expand your understanding and add to your skillset. The more you know, the more valuable you become—not just to yourself, but to others as well. Seek new opportunities to learn, and never be afraid to venture out of your comfort zone. Your growth as an individual sets you apart from others and solidifies your worth. Remember that knowledge is power, and your pursuit of it should be unrelenting. It is important to be grateful for what you have achieved, but past accomplishments should not hinder future progress. Use them as a stepping stone to reach even greater heights. Your achievements are not just reflections of your past efforts but also a testament to your future potential. Embrace your growth, and never be afraid to continue expanding your horizons. Your commitment to learning will not only benefit you, but it will also be an inspiration to those around you.

It's also important to understand that continuous learning is not just about gaining new knowledge or skills but also about growing as a person. When you invest time and effort into learning, you are not only expanding your understanding of the world but also increasing your self-awareness and developing your own values and beliefs. Personal growth can help you lead a more fulfilling life and be a better version of yourself, professionally and personally. By continuously learning, you are also increasing your value in the workforce. Companies and organizations are always looking for employees who are willing to continuously improve and develop their skills. By demonstrating an eagerness to do so, you can make yourself more attractive to potential employers and open up more opportunities for advancement in your career. Embracing the mindset of continuous learning can have a profound impact on your life, helping you achieve success and leading you down a path of growth and self-discovery.

ACTION STEPS:

- *Make learning a priority:* To make continuous learning a habit, it's important to prioritize it in your daily routine. This might mean setting aside specific times for learning, such as reading, watching educational videos, or making a commitment to take courses or attend workshops in your desired area of knowledge regularly. Make sure to choose engaging and interesting learning activities so you stay motivated.

- *Seek out diverse sources of knowledge:* To truly broaden your knowledge and perspective, it's important to seek out diverse sources of information. This might include reading books on various topics, listening to podcasts, attending lectures and seminars, or connecting with experts and mentors in your field. Try to seek out perspectives and ideas that challenge your assumptions and expand your thinking.

STAYING ON TRACK

Designation: Discipline, Goal Setting

LESSON:

It's important to understand that life is full of ups and downs, and it's natural to veer off track from goals at times. But it's crucial to recognize when this happens and not simply succumb to the routine of life and allow yourself to remain on autopilot. Instead, you must actively think about the steps you need to take to get back on track and continue toward your goals.

When you find yourself straying from your path, it's important to assess the situation and determine what steps you need to take in order to get back on track. This could mean reevaluating your goals, adjusting your strategies, or simply being more intentional with your actions. Whatever it is, it's essential to have a clear understanding of what needs to be done to continue moving forward. Once you have a plan in mind, the next step is to implement it. Integrating a plan into your routine requires discipline and a willingness to do the hard work necessary to achieve your goals. It may mean making sacrifices and working outside of your comfort zone, but in the end, it will be worth it. Consistent effort, dedication, and perseverance separate those who reach their goals from those who simply dream about them. So, when you are veering off track, embrace it as a challenge and take the necessary steps to get back on track and keep pushing forward.

ACTION STEPS:

- *Set clear goals:* Setting clear and specific goals is an important first step in staying on track. By knowing exactly what you want to achieve, you can create a plan of action and stay focused on the tasks that will help you reach your goals. Ensure your goals are realistic, measurable, and achievable within a specific time frame.
- *Develop a plan:* Once you have set your goals, develop a plan for achieving them. This might involve breaking your goals into smaller, more manageable tasks and creating a schedule or timeline for completing each task. A plan can help you stay focused and on track, even when things get challenging.
- *Monitor progress:* Regularly monitoring your progress is key to staying on track. This might involve tracking your progress toward your goals, keeping a journal to reflect on your experiences and challenges, or seeking feedback from others. By keeping tabs on your progress, you can make adjustments as needed and stay motivated and focused on the tasks at hand. Additionally, you can celebrate the progress made along the way as a way to further reinforce positive behaviour.

FAILURE—A PART OF LIFE

Designation: Resilience, Growth Mindset

LESSON:

Failure is an inevitable part of the human experience. It's important to understand that sometimes, despite our best efforts, things simply won't work out. It's easy to become discouraged when faced with setbacks and disappointments, but it's crucial to recognize that these experiences are opportunities for growth and learning. One of the key aspects of resilience is the ability to accept and embrace failure as a natural part of the journey. Instead of dwelling on your mistakes and shortcomings, focus on the lessons you can learn from each experience. What can you do differently next time? What did you learn about yourself? How can you use that knowledge to grow and improve?

It's also important to recognize that success is often the result of multiple failures and setbacks. It's only through trying, failing, and trying again that we can eventually achieve our goals. Each failure is simply a stepping stone on the path to success. Furthermore, it's essential to understand that sometimes, even with our best efforts, we simply can't control the outcome. Sometimes circumstances are beyond our power, and we must accept that and move on. By embracing the idea that failure is a natural part of the journey, we can develop the resilience and persistence needed to overcome obstacles and reach our goals. It's a fundamental principle of growth and self-improvement and one that should be embraced and celebrated, not feared or avoided.

ACTION STEPS:

- *Embrace a growth mindset:* The first step in understanding that failure is a part of life is to embrace a growth mindset. This involves viewing failure as an opportunity to learn and grow rather than viewing it as a negative outcome. By adopting a growth mindset, you can reframe your thinking around failure and see it as a necessary part of the learning process.
- *Practise self-compassion:* When you experience failure, it's important to practise self-compassion. Be kind and understanding to yourself, and acknowledge that failure is a natural part of the learning process. Instead of being overly critical or negative, focus on what you can learn from the experience and use it to inform your future actions.
- *Keep taking action:* Finally, to understand that failure is a part of life, it's important to keep taking action toward your goals. Remember that failure is not a reflection of your worth or potential, but simply a natural part of the process of growth and learning. Keep taking action, despite setbacks and failures, and focus on progress rather than outcomes. By doing so, you can continue to move forward, learn from your experiences, and grow as a person.

EMBRACING LOSSES AND WINS

Designation: Resilience, Growth Mindset

LESSON:

In life, we all experience losses and wins. Good times and the bad are an inevitable part of the journey, and it's important to embrace both. It's important to learn equally from both as well. Every loss or setback provides an opportunity to grow, learn, and become better, just as every win offers a chance to celebrate and recognize our achievements.

When we experience a loss, it's easy to feel discouraged and defeated, but it's crucial to see the loss as an opportunity for growth and learning. When you reflect on your losses, you can identify what went wrong and what you can do differently in future situations. This learning process will help you avoid making the same mistakes again and make you stronger and more resilient.

On the other hand, when you experience a win, it's essential to celebrate your achievements and acknowledge your hard work and dedication. In both losses and wins, it's important to keep a positive outlook and maintain a growth mindset where you understand that your abilities and intelligence can grow and develop over time. You believe every loss or setback is an opportunity to learn and improve, and you embrace challenges and failures as a natural part of the learning process. It's also important to remember that neither losses nor wins are permanent. Life is a continuous journey of ups and downs, and what may seem like a loss today may turn into a win in the future. Conversely, what may seem like a win today may turn into a loss in the future.

You cannot allow wins to go to your head, however. Remain humble and grounded, and recognize that your wins result from your efforts and the support of those around you. Staying humble through compliments is a crucial aspect of personal growth and success. Compliments are a powerful tool that can boost confidence and motivate us to continue toward our goals. When we receive compliments, it's easy to let our egos inflate, leading us to become arrogant and dismissive of others. This can result in a toxic cycle where we become so focused on ourselves that we lose sight of our purpose and those who have helped us along the way. To remain humble through compliments, it's important to acknowledge and appreciate the kind words but not let them define us. We should take compliments as an opportunity to reflect on our achievements and recognize the hard work and effort that went into them while not allowing them to become the driving force behind our actions.

Also, remember that success is not just about us. We must always be grateful for the support and help of others and recognize that our accomplishments are not solely our own. We must remain humble and acknowledge others who have played in our success, whether it's our family, friends, mentors, or colleagues. This allows us to continue learning and growing. When we are humble, we remain open to feedback and criticism, which can help us identify areas for improvement and continue on our path toward personal and professional growth. By acknowledging and appreciating compliments, remaining grateful for the support of others, and staying open to feedback and criticism, we can continue to learn, grow, and achieve our goals, all while maintaining a humble and grounded perspective.

ACTION STEPS:

- *Practise resilience:* Resilience is the ability to bounce back from setbacks and challenges, an important skill to cultivate when dealing with losses. To build resilience, focus on developing a growth mindset, practising self-care, and seeking social support. Remember that setbacks and challenges are a normal part of life and that with resilience, you can learn from your losses and come back even stronger.
- *Reflect and learn:* Whether you experience a loss or a win, it's important to take the time to reflect and learn from the experience. Ask yourself what you did well and what you

could have done better. Look for patterns and themes that emerge across different situations and use these insights to improve your future performance. Remember that every experience, whether positive or negative, can be an opportunity to learn and grow.

- ***Keep things in perspective:*** Finally, it's important to keep things in perspective. Avoid making sweeping generalizations based on a single experience, and try to view the situation in the larger context of your life. Remember that your self-worth is not determined by a single loss or win and that setbacks and successes are just one part of the journey.

MINDFULNESS OF THE SOURCE OF CRITICISM

Designation: Resilience, Self-Confidence

LESSON:

Don't let criticism get to your head—attempt to understand where it is coming from, whether it's a place of jealousy or sincere concern. Receiving criticism can be difficult, but it's important to approach it with an open mind and consider the motivation behind it. Some criticism may stem from jealousy or negativity, while other feedback may come from a place of genuine concern. Rather than allowing criticism to affect your self-esteem, try to understand the root of the criticism and determine whether it has any merit. This will help you to grow and improve rather than become defensive or discouraged. Additionally, evaluating criticism in this manner allows you to separate constructive feedback from negative comments, which can ultimately make you more resilient in the face of future criticism.

ACTION STEPS:

- *Stay objective:* When you receive criticism, try to remain objective and avoid taking it personally. Instead of seeing the criticism as an attack on you, focus on the specific actions or behaviours being criticized. This can help you see the criticism as constructive feedback rather than a personal insult.
- *Seek multiple perspectives:* Don't take one person's criticism as the definitive truth. Seek other perspectives and opinions, both positive and negative, to get a more well-rounded understanding of the situation. This can help you avoid getting too caught up in any one person's criticism and give you a more balanced perspective on the issue.
- *Use criticism as a learning opportunity:* Finally, try to use criticism as an opportunity to learn and grow. Instead of getting defensive or discouraged, ask yourself how you can use the feedback to improve your performance or behaviour. By using criticism constructively, you can turn it into a positive force in your life and work.

COMFORT IN DISCOMFORT

Designation: Resilience, Self-Improvement

LESSON:

Seeking comfort in discomfort is a mindset that can lead to personal growth and resilience. It involves embracing challenges and obstacles rather than avoiding them and recognizing the value that can be found in difficult experiences. This approach requires a willingness to embrace uncertainty and see difficulties as opportunities for growth and development.

One key to seeking comfort in discomfort is to create structure during chaos. Establishing a routine and a sense of stability can reduce stress levels and increase your ability to focus and perform. This structure can help you manage time and resources more effectively and use your energy and effort more efficiently. Another important aspect of seeking comfort in discomfort is to develop mental and emotional resilience. Curating resilience requires individuals to cultivate a positive outlook and to focus on the positive aspects of experiences, even when things are difficult. By learning to accept and embrace challenges, you can build resilience and increase your ability to bounce back from setbacks and adversity.

This mindset involves embracing the unknown and the uncertain. It requires an open mind to embrace new experiences, even if they may be challenging or uncomfortable. By creating structure amid chaos, developing mental and emotional resilience, and embracing the unknown, you can cultivate a mindset that will serve you well throughout your life.

ACTION STEPS:

- *Start small:* First, seek discomfort in small ways to build your resilience and tolerance for discomfort. For example, if you're usually very social, try spending an evening alone with your thoughts. If you're not used to public speaking, start speaking up more in small group settings before tackling a larger audience. Gradually increasing your exposure to discomfort can help you build the mental and emotional strength you need to tackle more significant challenges.
- *Reframe your mindset:* Instead of seeing discomfort as something to avoid or fear, try reframing it as an opportunity for growth and learning. Embrace the challenges that

come your way, and focus on the lessons you can learn from them. This shift in mindset can help you feel more empowered and less anxious when facing uncomfortable situations.
- *Practise mindfulness:* Mindfulness techniques like meditation and deep breathing can help you manage the physical and emotional discomfort that often comes with challenging situations. By focusing on your breath and staying present in the moment, you can reduce stress and anxiety and remain centered and calm even in discomfort.

IMPORTANCE OF PATIENCE

Designation: Patience, Resilience, Personal Growth, Communication

LESSON:

Practise patience in all aspects of life. Be patient with people who you're working for or who are working for you. Keep a calm demeanour around those you deal with day to day. Practising patience in all aspects of life is a critical component of success and personal growth. When you're patient with others, you demonstrate your ability to understand and respect perspectives, even when they may be different from your own. This can help to build strong relationships and foster a positive and productive work or life environment. In high-pressure situations, it can be tempting to make impulsive decisions without fully considering all options and outcomes. However, taking a step back and allowing time to calm down and reflect can help you make more informed and thoughtful decisions. This can help you avoid rash decisions that may have negative consequences in the long run.

Being patient in your daily interactions can also help improve your overall well-being. By maintaining a calm demeanour and recognizing what needs to be done right away and what can wait, you're reducing your stress levels and allowing yourself to approach each situation with a clear mind. This can lead to a more positive and fulfilling experience in your personal and professional life. This trait can also be important for personal development and growth. Often, the things that have the most significant impact and bring the most satisfaction take time and effort to achieve. You need to be patient with yourself, recognize that progress takes time, and understand that setbacks are just temporary.

Instead of getting discouraged at times, use these as opportunities to learn and improve. It's also important to remember that people come from different backgrounds, have different perspectives and experiences, and process information differently. By approaching others with patience and understanding, you can better understand where they're coming from and find common ground. This can lead to stronger relationships and more effective communication, both essential aspects of life. So, cultivate patience and apply it to all areas of your life, and you'll see positive results in the long run.

ACTION STEPS:

- *Practise mindfulness:* Mindfulness meditation can help you develop patience by teaching you to focus on the present moment and observe your thoughts and feelings without judgment. This practise can help you stay calm and centered in difficult situations.
- *Embrace the process:* Remember that developing patience is a process that will take time to see results. Be patient with

yourself, embrace the process, and celebrate small victories along the way.
- *Cultivate gratitude:* Practising gratitude can help you develop patience by shifting your focus away from what you don't have and toward what you do have. Take time each day to reflect on the things you are grateful for.

> **Note:** Since this word will be mentioned more throughout this book, it's worth a deeper explanation.
>
> What is gratitude? Gratitude is the practise of appreciating and valuing yourself for who you are and being thankful for your efforts and accomplishments. It's a positive and compassionate relationship with yourself that fosters self-esteem and personal growth.
>
> In simpler terms, gratitude is appreciating what you are and what you have while remembering where you came from. Although things can always be better, they can always get significantly worse. You are here today. Be grateful for that.

FACING PROBLEMS

Designation: Resilience, Forward Thinking

LESSON:

It is important to face our problems head-on and not allow them to fester and grow into larger, less manageable issues. Ignoring problems will not make them disappear; instead, they will only linger and possibly intensify. This can lead to a sense of guilt and feeling overwhelmed until we eventually face the task. By confronting problems, we not only remove that overwhelming feeling, but we can also gain a sense of satisfaction from having accomplished something we previously dreaded. This can lead to an increase in self-confidence and a feeling of empowerment. It is important to remember that the longer we avoid a problem, the harder it will become to face and solve.

It is human nature to avoid confronting difficult or unpleasant situations, but by facing our challenges, we demonstrate self-discipline and determination that is essential to personal growth and success. Whether it is a task at work, a difficult conversation with a loved one, or a personal goal that we have been putting off, taking action toward resolving the issue is crucial. In some cases, the outcome may not be what we had hoped for, but the simple act of facing the problem and taking steps toward a resolution can provide relief and a newfound sense of control over the situation.

It's important to remember that problems do not solve themselves—they only grow and compound over time. By approaching challenges with a sense of purpose and determination, we can resolve the issue at hand and gain valuable experience and knowledge that will serve us well in future challenges.

ACTION STEPS:
- *Identify the problem:* The first step in facing problems head-on is to identify the problem. Take the time to clearly define what the problem is and what the underlying issues may be. Be specific and focus on the facts.
- *Develop a plan:* Once you have identified the problem, develop an action plan. Determine the steps you need to take to address the problem and consider potential solutions. Break the plan into smaller, actionable steps to make it more manageable.
- *Take action:* Finally, take action. Follow through on your developed plan and take the necessary steps to address the

problem. Be prepared to adjust your approach as needed and be open to feedback from others. Taking action can help build confidence and momentum, making it easier to face future problems head-on.

EVERYONE STRUGGLES

Designation: Resilience, Overcoming Adversity

LESSON:

It is a common misconception to believe that some people have an easy life while others face constant struggles and hardships. The truth is that everyone experiences their own unique set of challenges, setbacks, and difficulties in life, regardless of their background or circumstances. It can be easy to fall into the trap of comparing our lives to those around us, especially in the age of social media, where people often portray a carefully curated image of their lives. However, the reality is that nobody's life is perfect, and we all have our struggles and battles to fight.

Recognizing this fact is essential for our personal growth and development. When we understand that everyone has their own challenges, we can start to view our struggles as a normal part of the human experience. This can help us approach our challenges with a more positive and proactive mindset rather than feeling like we are the only ones facing difficulties.

It's important to remember that everyone experiences highs and lows throughout their lives. We all have moments of success and happiness, as well as moments of disappointment and despair. The key to achieving a fulfilling life is not to avoid challenges and hardships altogether but to develop the resilience and mindset necessary to navigate them with grace and determination. When we remember that nobody has an easy life, we can create a greater sense of empathy and compassion toward others. We can recognize that everyone is doing their best with their resources, and that we all deserve love, respect, and understanding.

ACTION STEPS:

- *Practise empathy:* It can be helpful to try to put yourself in other people's shoes and understand what they might be going through. This can help you develop empathy and compassion, which can be helpful in your struggles as well. When you realize that others have struggles too, it can be comforting to know that you are not alone.
- *Focus on gratitude:* Practising gratitude can help you shift your focus from what's not going well to what is going well. Make a list of things you are grateful for, no matter how small they may seem. This can help you stay positive and see the good things in your life, even during a difficult time.
- *Seek support:* It's important to seek support when going through a difficult time. This can be from friends, family, a support group, or a therapist. Having someone to talk to and support you can make a big difference. It's also important to remember that asking for help is a sign of strength, not weakness. There is less strength in solitude.

NONACCEPTANCE OF FAILING TRAITS

Designation: Self-Improvement, Personal Growth, Limiting Beliefs

LESSON:

The minute you accept that you cannot do something is the minute you determine you will never be able to do that thing. The mindset you adopt has a powerful impact on your ability to achieve your goals. When you believe you are capable of something, you are more likely to put in the effort and make the necessary sacrifices to make it happen. Additionally, if you believe you cannot do something, you are more likely to give up before even trying. This limiting belief becomes a self-fulfilling prophecy, as you are less likely to take action or push yourself beyond your comfort zone.

The same is true for your physical abilities. The human body is capable of remarkable things, but many people limit their potential by believing they are not strong, fast, flexible, or young enough. However, with proper training, nutrition, and mindset, your body can be transformed and pushed to achieve things that you once thought were impossible. Therefore, it is crucial to adopt a growth mindset and believe that you have the potential to achieve your goals, no matter how challenging they may seem. Whether it is a physical or mental challenge, never give up. Instead, believe in yourself, work hard, and focus on your goals. With perseverance, you can overcome obstacles and achieve greatness.

ACTION STEPS:

- *Reframe your mindset:* The first step to countering the mentality of accepting you cannot do something is to reframe your mindset. Instead of telling yourself that you cannot do something, try telling yourself that you have not *yet* succeeded. This subtle shift in mindset can help you to approach the challenge with a more positive and growth-oriented attitude.
- *Challenge limiting beliefs:* Identify the negative beliefs holding you back and challenge them. Ask yourself, "Is this belief true?" and "What evidence do I have to support it?"
- *Seek out resources:* Don't be afraid to seek resources and support to help you achieve your goals. This can include things like books, videos, courses, mentors, or coaches.
- *Practise, practise, practise:* Practise is key to developing new skills and abilities. Set aside time each day to work on the skill you want to improve, even if it's just for a few minutes.
- *Reframe failure as an opportunity:* Failure is a natural part of the learning process. Instead of viewing failure as a setback, reframe it as an opportunity to learn and grow. Ask yourself, "What can I learn from this experience?" and "How can I use this knowledge to improve in the future?"

IF IT IS OVER, DON'T DWELL ON IT. LEARN FROM IT.

Designation: Resilience, Self-Improvement

LESSON:

When something is over, it's important to not dwell on it and instead focus on learning from the experience. Dwelling on past mistakes or missed opportunities can be a futile exercise that only keeps you stuck in the past. This can prevent you from moving forward and learning from the situation, thus repeating the same mistakes in the future.

However, learning from past experiences is crucial to personal growth and development. It allows individuals to reflect on what went well and what could have been done differently and to use that knowledge to make better decisions in the future. This type of introspection can lead to the formation of new insights, perspectives, and ways of thinking, which can help individuals grow and evolve. Furthermore, it's essential to recognize that failures, mistakes, and missed opportunities are a natural part of life. They provide valuable lessons and experiences that can help individuals grow and develop. Instead of dwelling on the negative aspects of a situation, focus on the positive lessons that you can learn from it. This mindset shift can help individuals approach challenges and obstacles with a more positive and proactive attitude, leading to greater success and fulfilment in the long run. It can also help individuals grow and evolve, leading to greater success and satisfaction in the future. Embrace failures, mistakes, and missed opportunities as opportunities for learning and growth, and use them as a stepping stone toward a better future.

ACTION STEPS:

- ***Reflect on the experience:*** Take time to reflect on the experience and what you can learn from it. This might involve journaling, talking to a trusted friend or therapist, or simply spending quiet time alone to process your thoughts and feelings. Ask yourself what went well, what could have been better, and what you can do differently in the future.
- ***Focus on the present:*** While learning from past experiences

is important, it's equally important to stay present and focused on the here and now. Instead of dwelling on what could have been, focus on what you can do today to move forward. This might involve setting new goals, taking positive action toward your dreams, or simply enjoying the moment and being grateful for what you have.
- *Let go of regrets:* Finally, it's important to let go of regrets and forgive yourself for any mistakes you may have made. Remember that everyone makes mistakes and that the most important thing is how you respond to them. By accepting responsibility for your actions, learning from your experiences, and moving forward with a positive attitude, you can create a brighter, more fulfilling future for yourself.

YOU CANNOT PLEASE EVERYONE ALL THE TIME

Designation: Setting Realistic Expectations, Forward Thinking

LESSON:

It's a universal truth that you can't please everyone all the time. No matter how hard you try, there will always be someone who disagrees with you or is dissatisfied with your decisions. In these situations, it's important to weigh your options and consider what's best for you and your future or the future of your group or company. When faced with a decision, take the time to consider all angles and weigh the pros and cons. Don't make decisions based solely on what others want or expect of you. Instead, consider what aligns with your values, goals, and priorities and what will bring you the most significant long-term benefits.

It's also important to consider the impact of your decisions on others, especially regarding the future of a group or company. In these situations, it's important to balance the needs and desires of different stakeholders and make decisions that will ultimately benefit everyone involved. Remember, making decisions that are best for you and your future, or the future of a group or company, requires courage and conviction. Don't be afraid to stand up for your beliefs and make decisions that will ultimately lead to success and fulfilment. By doing so, you'll develop a reputation for integrity and leadership and set yourself on a path toward success and satisfaction.

ACTION STEPS:

- *Identify your values:* It's important to identify your values and priorities and to use them as a guide when making decisions. When you know what's important to you, it's easier to make choices that align with those values, even if they don't please everyone. By being true to yourself and your values, you'll be more confident in your decisions and less likely to be swayed by others' opinions.
- *Learn to say no:* Saying no can be difficult, but it's an important skill to master to avoid overcommitting yourself and pleasing everyone. When someone asks you to do something that doesn't align with your values or priorities, it's okay to decline politely. You don't have to offer an elaborate excuse or apology—a simple "No, thank you" will do. By setting boundaries and being firm in your decisions, you'll be more respected by others and more confident in your abilities.
- *Seek feedback selectively:* It's important to seek feedback from others to grow and improve, but it's equally important to be selective of sources of feedback. Not everyone's opinion is equally valuable or relevant to your goals and values.

Instead of seeking feedback from everyone, be strategic and seek feedback from people with expertise or experience in the area you're looking to improve. By being selective about feedback, you'll be less likely to be swayed by others' opinions that may not be helpful or relevant to your situation.

DON'T LET OTHERS HOLD YOU BACK

Designation: Personal Empowerment

LESSON:

Don't let others slow or stop you from achieving your goal. Not everyone will have the same mindset as you, and that's alright. Success in any form comes to those who put in the work. It is essential to understand that not everyone will have the same drive, ambition, or vision as you do. While it can be disheartening to see others not working toward the same goals, or any goals for that matter, it is important to remember that success comes to those who do the work. You must focus on your journey and not let the actions of others slow you down or hold you back.

When you put in the effort, you open yourself to a world of possibilities. People who are successful and achieve their goals are the ones who are willing to do what it takes. They understand that success is not handed out but earned through hard work and dedication. So, don't let others discourage you or make you believe you are not good enough. Focus on your goal and the path to get there. Surround yourself with positive, supportive people who encourage and motivate you. And most importantly, never stop trying to reach your goal. The reward for success is worth it all.

ACTION STEPS:

- *Stay focused on your goals:* Keep your goals in mind and focus on the things that matter most to you. This can help you stay motivated and on track, even when others are trying to distract you or steer you off course. Be clear about your priorities and make decisions that align with your goals.
- *Set boundaries:* If there are people in your life who are distracting or discouraging you from your goals, it's important to set boundaries. This might involve limiting the amount of time you spend with certain people or being clear about what you are willing and not willing to do. Be assertive in communicating your boundaries, and don't hesitate to say no when necessary.
- *Surround yourself with supportive people:* This can help you stay motivated and focused on your goals. Seek friends, family members, or colleagues who share your values and can offer encouragement and support.

YOU DON'T KNOW IF YOU DON'T TRY

Designation: New Opportunities, Taking Risks

LESSON:

You don't know if you don't try. Consider the example of seeking a higher position in your employment: attempt to speak to those in similar positions to the one you want or ones who previously held the title. In doing so, you can gain valuable insights and advice to help you reach your own career goals. You'd be surprised how many people are willing to help, although some will protect that information for fear of being outshined. Despite this, it is still worth making an effort to reach out and make connections, as the potential benefits are substantial. To achieve these goals, it is essential to take proactive steps and engage in meaningful conversations with others who have already achieved what you desire.

It is important to note that not everyone will be willing to share their knowledge and experience with you. Some individuals may choose to protect their information and expertise for fear of being surpassed by others. The journey toward greater success and fulfilment in one's career is not always easy, but by taking bold steps and seeking the wisdom of others, you can build the foundation for a bright future. So, go ahead and try. You never know what you may achieve until you take that first step.

ACTION STEPS:

- *Embrace the idea of experimentation:* To adopt a mindset of this lesson, it is important to embrace the idea of experimentation. Rather than being afraid to try new things, approach them as opportunities. Be willing to take risks and try new approaches, even if they don't always achieve the desired outcome.
- *Focus on learning from failure:* Failure can be a powerful learning opportunity. Rather than seeing it as a sign of weakness, approach failure as a chance to learn and grow. Analyze what went wrong, and identify what you can do differently in the future. This can help you approach new challenges with greater confidence and resilience.
- *Challenge limiting beliefs:* Often, we avoid trying new things because of limiting beliefs we hold about ourselves or our abilities. Ask yourself if there's evidence to support them and, if not, try to reframe them in a more positive and

empowering way. This can help you overcome self-doubt and approach new challenges with greater openness and curiosity.

"I WISH" STATEMENTS

Designation: Productivity, Mindset, Goal Setting

LESSON:

The problem with "I wish" statements is that they remain just that: wishes. They are expressions of desire, but without concrete action and effort, they are unlikely to become reality. To achieve your goals, you must be proactive and take concrete steps to make them happen. It's easy to get stuck in the cycle of dreaming and wishing, but unless you are willing to put in the work and make sacrifices, your desires will remain just that. To achieve your goals, you must have a clear vision, set specific and measurable objectives, and create an action plan.

Furthermore, it's essential to understand that success doesn't come overnight. It requires consistent effort, discipline, and a willingness to take calculated risks. You must be willing to put in the time and effort to build the skills, knowledge, and resources necessary to reach your goals. You must also be ready to be held accountable for your actions. That means keeping track of your progress, reviewing your strategies regularly, and making adjustments as needed. By doing so, you can stay on track and avoid the pitfalls that sabotage your progress.

To achieve your goals, you must be willing to take action, be persistent, and stay focused. Dreams are wonderful, but they are only the first step. To make them a reality, you must take the necessary steps to turn them into tangible outcomes.

ACTION STEPS:

- **Reframe your thinking:** The first step in addressing the problem with "I wish" statements is to reframe your thinking. Instead of focusing on what you wish you could do, focus on what actions you can take to achieve your goals. This can help shift your mindset from a passive one to an active one and empower you to take control of your life.
- **Set achievable goals:** To avoid getting stuck in a cycle of "I wish" statements, it's important to set achievable goals. Identify specific, measurable goals that you can work toward and break them down into manageable steps. This can help you stay motivated and focused and make it easier to act rather than simply wishing for something to happen.
- **Take action:** Finally, to avoid the problem of "I wish" statements, it's important to take action. Start with those small, manageable steps, and build momentum over time. Whether you're signing up for a course, applying for a job, or taking appropriate measures to save for that amazing vacation or dream home, take action toward your goals and avoid getting stuck in a cycle of wishing and hoping. Remember that progress takes time, and small steps taken consistently can add up to larger results over time.

PERSISTENCE

Designation: Persistence, Productivity, Achieving Goals

LESSON:

When faced with a difficult situation, it's easy to feel discouraged and give up. Persistence is key to overcoming obstacles and finding solutions. In business and life, it's important to approach challenges with a positive attitude and a determination to find a way forward. One of the primary considerations in persistence is to focus on finding alternative solutions. When faced with a problem, it's easy to get stuck in a single way of thinking and assume that there is only one possible solution. But in reality, there are often many different ways to approach a problem, and many different solutions can work. By exploring different options and being creative, individuals can often find a solution that works for everyone involved.

Another important aspect of persistence is to engage with the other people involved in the situation. By asking questions and seeking input and feedback, individuals can build a collaborative environment that is more likely to lead to a positive outcome. This also involves having open and honest conversations about what is possible and what is not, and working together to find a way forward. Where possible, it's important to focus on finding a solution that works for everyone. In a business setting, this might mean looking for a win–win scenario that benefits both parties. In personal relationships, aim to find a solution that meets everyone's needs and addresses everyone's concerns. By taking a collaborative approach, individuals can build trust and establish long-lasting relationships that will serve them well in the future. By embracing challenges and seeking creative solutions, individuals can grow and develop in ways they never thought possible.

ACTION STEPS:
- *Set clear goals:* Knowing what you want to achieve and having a plan in place can help you stay focused and motivated. Set *s*pecific, *m*easurable, *a*chievable, *r*elevant, and *t*ime-bound (**SMART**) goals that are challenging but real-

istic. Write them down and monitor your progress to stay on track.
- **Develop a growth mindset:** Cultivate a belief that you can learn and grow from your failures and setbacks. Embrace challenges as opportunities to learn and try again rather than as signs of your limitations. This can help you stay persistent and motivated even in the face of obstacles.
- **Break down large tasks:** If your goal is particularly daunting, break it down into smaller, more manageable steps. This can help you avoid feeling overwhelmed and give you a sense of progress as you complete each step. Celebrate small successes along the way to stay motivated.
- **Ask the right questions:** If a client or company representative tells you that a deal cannot go through or they can't make something happen, don't be afraid to ask why and say, "What can we do to make this work?" or "What would we need to make this happen?" The power of that suggestion can go a long way.

FOCUS ON WORK-RELATED TASKS

Designation: Productivity, Time Management

LESSON:

In any line of work, repetitive and frequently performed tasks are the foundation of your responsibilities. Neglecting or performing these tasks inadequately will quickly paint a picture of your work ethic and capabilities in the eyes of those around you. You must approach even the most mundane tasks with the same level of purpose and dedication as the new, uncharted responsibilities that may come your way. Doing so establishes a standard of excellence that showcases your competence and commitment to your responsibilities. In time, when you are trusted with more challenging and less frequent tasks, your coworkers, colleagues, and superiors will have confidence in your ability to complete them effectively. If, however, they see that you have not upheld the standard on daily tasks, they are less likely to trust your judgment and ability when it comes to the more complex and nonroutine tasks.

One must understand that the most seemingly insignificant tasks can nonetheless have a major impact. Performing even the most basic of tasks with care, attention, and diligence can set a standard for those around you, inspire and encourage those with whom you work, and demonstrate your character and work ethic. In this manner, even the most basic tasks can be a stepping stone to greater success, accomplishment, and recognition. Therefore, focus on completing even the simplest of tasks to the best of your ability every time. This approach sets a bar for excellence, making it clear to those around you that you are not only competent, but also dedicated to your responsibilities and that you approach every aspect of your work with the same level of commitment and attention to detail.

ACTION STEPS:
- *Prioritize your tasks:* To complete work tasks effectively, it's important to prioritize them. Identify the most important tasks to be completed first and create a plan for completing them. This can help you stay organized and focused and ensure you're using your time and energy effectively.
- *Break tasks into smaller parts:* When faced with an enormous task, it can be overwhelming and challenging to know where to start. One strategy to help you overcome this is to

break the task down into smaller, more manageable parts. This can help you feel more in control of the task and make it easier to stay focused and motivated.
- *Use time management techniques:* Time management techniques can help complete work tasks efficiently. For example, the *Pomodoro Technique* involves working for twenty-five-minute intervals followed by short breaks, which can help you stay focused and avoid burnout. Additionally, creating a schedule for your workday can help you stay on track and ensure that you're making progress toward completing your tasks.

EXPENDING ENERGY

Designation: Time Management, Efficiency, Productivity

LESSON:

Properly expending energy is a critical component of success in any area of life. Whether you are striving for career success, pursuing a hobby or passion, or working to improve your health and well-being, managing your energy will play a key role in determining your progress and ultimate success. One of the steps to expending energy properly is to prioritize and focus on what is most important. This means taking the time to identify your core goals and values and directing your energy toward those areas that will have the greatest impact on achieving those objectives. It may also mean learning to say no to other activities or commitments that do not align with your priorities or may drain your energy unnecessarily.

Another important element of expending energy properly is recognizing the importance of rest and recovery. While it may be tempting to push yourself to the limit daily, doing so can lead to burnout, injury, or other setbacks that can derail your progress. Instead, it is important to build rest and recovery time into your routine, whether taking regular breaks during the day, prioritizing sleep and relaxation, or taking time off to recharge your batteries.

Additionally, this means being mindful of the resources you have available to you, whether those are financial resources, social support, or other forms of assistance. By strategically leveraging your resources, you can optimize your energy expenditure and increase your chances of success in whatever pursuit you are undertaking.

ACTION STEPS:

- *Identify your most important goals:* Take time to reflect on what is most important to you and what you want to achieve. Make a list of your goals and prioritize them based on their importance. By focusing your energy on the goals that matter most, you'll be able to make progress more efficiently and effectively.
- *Use time management techniques:* Good time management can help you conserve your energy by working smarter, not harder. Use techniques such as the *Pomodoro* Technique (mentioned above) to break your workday into focused sprints with breaks in between. This can help you stay energized and focused throughout the day.
- *Practise self-care:* Taking care of your physical, emotional, and mental well-being can help you conserve energy in the long run. Make sure to get enough sleep, eat a healthy diet, exercise regularly, and take breaks when you need them. You can also practise stress-reducing techniques, such as

meditation, yoga, or deep breathing, to help you stay centered and energized.

ALIGNING INTERESTS WITH PRODUCTIVITY

Designation: Productivity, Passion, Purpose

LESSON:

One of the key factors to success and satisfaction in life is the alignment of personal interests with productive activities. When our interests and pursuits align with our work and goals, we are more likely to be motivated and engaged and experience a sense of fulfilment and purpose. However, aligning our interests with our productive endeavours is not always easy. Sometimes our interests may be too narrowly defined or may not have a clear path for turning them into a productive pursuit. In other cases, our interests may be at odds with our work or the demands of daily life.

The key to aligning interests with productivity is to start with a deep understanding of your own interests, values, and strengths. This requires taking the time to reflect on what truly drives and motivates you and identify the areas where you feel the most fulfilled and engaged. Once we have a clear understanding of our interests and motivations, we can explore ways to integrate them into our work and life in general. This may involve seeking new opportunities, developing new skills, or changing careers if necessary. Remember that this process may take time and involve some trial and error. The key is to stay focused on aligning our interests with our productivity and to be open to new experiences and challenges along the way.

By aligning our interests and productivity, we can create a

rich, fulfilling, and meaningful life that allows us to make the most of the time we have. Whether through our work, hobbies, or relationships, when we are doing what we love, we can tap into a wellspring of energy, creativity, and passion that can drive us forward and help us achieve great things.

ACTION STEPS:

- *Identify your interests:* Start by identifying the things that interest you and ignite your passion—anything from hobbies to career aspirations. Consider what motivates and excites you and what you would enjoy doing. Write them down if need be.
- *Find ways to incorporate your interests into your work:* Once you have identified your interests, look for ways to incorporate them into your work. This could involve finding a job or career that aligns with your interests or finding ways to bring your interests into your current work. For example, if you are interested in graphic design, you could find ways to incorporate design elements into your presentations or reports.
- *Set goals and track progress:* Setting goals can help you stay motivated and focused on aligning your interests with productivity. Set specific and achievable goals, and track your progress over time. This can help you see an impact and help you stay on track when faced with challenges or setbacks. Celebrate your successes along the way, and use them to motivate yourself to continue aligning your interests with productivity.

OBJECTS IN MOTION STAY IN MOTION

Designation: Productivity, Taking Action, Momentum

LESSON:

"Objects in motion stay in motion; objects at rest stay at rest." This is a fundamental principle of physics known as Newton's First Law of Motion. But it can also be applied to one's personal life and mindset. Just like an object in motion continues to move unless acted upon by an outside force, the same goes for our actions and habits. When we are consistently in motion, putting in effort, and taking action toward our goals, we are more likely to continue making progress.

On the other hand, if we fall into a state of rest and inactivity, it can be difficult to get back into motion and make headway. It is important to understand our actions, habits, and mindset all have a compounding effect, and it is up to us to choose to stay in motion and continue pushing toward our goals.

ACTION STEPS:

- *Set clear goals:* When you have a clear idea of where you want to go and what you want to achieve, it's easier to maintain momentum and stay in motion. Make sure your goals are specific, measurable, and achievable, and break them down into smaller steps to help you stay on track.
- *Establish good habits:* Start small and work on building one habit at a time. Whether going for a daily walk, practising meditation, or working on a creative project for a set amount of time each day, find habits that align with your goals and make them a part of your routine.
- *Stay motivated:* It's sometimes easier said than done, but

staying motivated is key to maintaining momentum. Find sources of inspiration and motivation that resonate with you, whether reading inspiring quotes, listening to uplifting music, or surrounding yourself with supportive friends and family members. The best motivation comes from within and drives you to reach long-term goals.

- *Stay accountable:* Lastly, staying accountable to yourself and others can help you stay in motion. Find an accountability partner, whether a friend, family member, or coach, who can help keep you on track and offer support and encouragement. Even telling a friend or posting on social media can push you to be true to your word. Track your progress and celebrate your successes together, and work together to overcome any challenges that arise along the way.

Everyone's journey is unique, and the success you create is yours to claim.

II.

TEAMWORK, RELATIONSHIPS

"If you are not willing to be a fool, you can't become a master."
—JORDAN B. PETERSON

WELCOME TO A NEW CHAPTER IN YOUR JOURNEY TOWARD success. Life is a complex web of relationships and interactions, and your ability to navigate and thrive in this interconnected world is crucial to your personal and professional success. In this chapter, we will explore two essential themes—Teamwork and Relationships—that play a pivotal role in unlocking your potential and achieving greatness.

Teamwork is about harnessing the power of collaboration and working together toward a common goal. It's about leveraging the strengths and abilities of others to achieve more than what you could on your own. In today's fast-paced and competitive world, working effectively with others is a critical skill. Effective teamwork can drive success and create lasting impact, whether in your workplace, community, or personal life. Through the principles, strategies, and practical tips in this chapter, you will learn how to build high-performing teams, foster a culture of trust and accountability, and achieve collective success.

Relationships are the cornerstone of our lives. They bring joy, fulfilment, and a sense of belonging. Strong relationships are built on trust, respect, and effective communication. They provide support, guidance, and opportunities for growth. In today's interconnected world, cultivating meaningful relationships is more important than ever. Whether it's with your family, friends, colleagues, or mentors, strong relationships can enrich your life and open doors to new opportunities. Through the insights, strategies, and practical guidance in this chapter, you will learn how to create a positive support network, cultivate long-lasting friendships, and navigate challenges with grace and integrity.

As you embark on this journey exploring the power of teamwork and relationships, I will provide valuable insights and actionable steps to apply these principles in your daily life. Through real-life examples, practical exercises, and relatable stories, you will gain the tools and mindset needed to foster positive connections, build strong teams, and achieve success in all aspects of life. I understand that change can be challenging and navigating the complexities of teamwork and relationships may not always be easy, but the rewards are immeasurable. By mastering these essential life skills, you will be equipped with the mindset and strategies needed to overcome challenges, build meaningful connections, and achieve success in your personal and professional endeavours.

In the following chapter, we will dive deep into the principles, strategies, and practical steps to harness the power of teamwork and relationships in your life. So, get ready to unlock your potential, cultivate meaningful connections, and achieve greatness. The journey continues.

EVERYONE HAS SOMETHING TO OFFER

Designation: Teamwork, Collaboration

LESSON:

It's important to remember that everyone has something to offer, regardless of age or experience. Being open to guidance from those who are older and younger than you can broaden your perspective and help you see things in a new light. This can help you to continue growing and developing both personally and professionally. Humbling yourself and admitting that you don't know everything is a sign of strength, not weakness. This can be especially true when seeking advice from someone with a different life experience or perspective. You never know what valuable insights they may have to offer.

We all assume age is an indicator of wisdom, which may be true but is not always the case. It may feel strange to take advice from someone five, ten, twenty, or thirty years younger than you, but maybe there's a chance they see something from an angle you don't. Or perhaps they've experienced something you haven't. The only way to find out is to listen and apply it to your life or current situation.

Additionally, by actively seeking guidance from a diverse range of individuals, you demonstrate a willingness to learn and grow. This can be especially beneficial in a fast-paced and constantly changing world, where staying ahead of the curve and adapting to new challenges is important. So, don't be afraid to ask for advice, and take the time to listen and consider the opinions of others. It can be a valuable tool in your ongoing journey toward personal and professional growth.

ACTION STEPS:

- *Listen actively:* Give others the space to share their ideas and perspectives. Ask questions, seek clarification, and show genuine interest in what they say. This will help you better understand their strengths and how they can contribute to a situation or problem.
- *Look for strengths in others:* Recognize their unique talents and abilities. Be on the lookout for what others do well, and acknowledge and celebrate their successes. Doing so will help to create a positive and supportive environment and encourage others to share their strengths and talents.
- *Create opportunities for collaboration:* Bring people together to work toward a common goal. Encourage others to share their ideas and perspectives and work together to solve problems. By collaborating with others, you can leverage their strengths and create a more effective and innovative outcome.
- *Be open-minded:* Finally, be open-minded and willing to learn from others. Recognize that everyone has something to offer, and consider new ideas and perspectives. By being open-minded, you can broaden your horizons and gain new insights and knowledge from others.

TEAM STRENGTHS AND WEAKNESSES

Designation: Teamwork, Leadership

LESSON:

As a leader, it is important to understand the strengths and weaknesses of those with whom you work. By assigning tasks that play to their strengths, you are setting them up for success and increasing your team's overall efficiency and effectiveness. On the other hand, working on weaknesses through training can help individuals improve and grow in their roles. This approach benefits not only the individual, but also the team as a whole by utilizing each member's unique skills and abilities to the fullest. In this way, a leader can create a positive and productive work environment where everyone can contribute to the best of their abilities.

The idea behind this approach is that individuals are more likely to perform at their best when working in an area where they are naturally skilled. When tasks align with their strengths, they can draw on their inherent abilities and produce better results. The team or organization can achieve greater success and efficiency by focusing on each person's strengths. You can address weaknesses through training and development, allowing individuals to improve over time. This approach also helps foster a sense of engagement and satisfaction among team members, as they feel valued and utilized. By aligning tasks with strengths, leaders can create a work environment that is both productive and enjoyable for everyone.

ACTION STEPS:

- *Conduct a team assessment:* One effective way to identify team strengths and weaknesses is to conduct a team assessment. This can involve gathering feedback from team members through surveys or interviews, assessing team performance metrics, and evaluating team dynamics. Use this information to create a profile of your team's strengths and weaknesses.
- *Leverage individual strengths:* Once you've identified your team's strengths, find ways to leverage them. Assign team members to tasks that play to their strengths and allow them to share their expertise with others. This can help to build morale and create a sense of ownership and investment in the team's success. Additionally, address your team's weaknesses by developing training or other support initiatives to improve skills and performance, which will help create a more well-rounded team.

MULTIPLE MINDS AND INPUTS

Designation: Teamwork, Collaboration

LESSON:

It is a common misconception that individual genius can solve most problems. The reality is that collective minds have a wealth of experience, knowledge, and expertise that cannot be achieved by one person alone. To take advantage of the group's wisdom, it is important to listen to the thoughts and ideas of others. This means being open to their input and actively seeking and considering it in your decision-making process. By doing so, you open yourself up to new perspectives and ways of thinking, leading to better outcomes and more successful problem-solving. Additionally, by working with others, you can tap into their areas of expertise and specialize in your own. This allows for greater efficiency as you can delegate tasks to those best equipped to handle them. By pooling your resources, you can achieve far more than you could alone.

It is important to remember that everyone brings their own unique skills, experiences, and perspectives. By considering these, you can gain a more complete picture of any given situation and make decisions that are informed by a wide range of opinions and insights. In this way, collective minds can be a powerful tool for problem-solving and success.

ACTION STEPS:

- *Seek out diverse perspectives:* When seeking multiple minds and inputs, it's important to seek diverse perspectives. This might mean engaging with people with different backgrounds, experiences, and viewpoints or actively seeking views that challenge your own assumptions and biases. By seeking diverse perspectives, you'll gain a more well-rounded understanding of the topic at hand and be better equipped to make informed decisions.
- *Encourage open communication:* To leverage multiple minds and inputs effectively, it's important to encourage open communication. This means creating a space where people feel comfortable sharing their ideas, concerns, and feedback and actively soliciting input from all stakeholders. By encouraging open communication, you'll foster a culture of collaboration and build trust and buy-in among your team.
- *Establish a decision-making process:* Finally, when leveraging multiple minds and inputs, it's important to establish a

decision-making process that takes all input into account. This might involve establishing criteria for decision-making, creating a framework for weighing different options and perspectives, and empowering decision-makers to make informed choices. By establishing a straightforward decision-making process, you'll be better equipped to take advantage of multiple minds and inputs and make informed decisions that your team supports.

"WE" INSTEAD OF "ME"

Designation: Teamwork, Leadership

LESSON:

The use of "we" versus "me" can have a significant impact on team dynamics and the way success or failure is perceived and handled. In a team setting, it is important to focus on the collective effort and give credit where it is due. When celebrating successes, acknowledge the contributions of everyone involved and use "we" language instead of "me." This approach helps build morale and creates a sense of camaraderie among team members. It also fosters a culture of teamwork and collaboration, which is essential for achieving long-term success. Alternatively, when admitting failures or shortcomings, it is equally important to take personal responsibility and use "me" instead of "them." This shows a willingness to accept accountability and work to resolve the issue. By doing so, individuals can learn from their mistakes and make improvements, which will ultimately contribute to the success of the team as a whole.

This shift in thinking also helps create a culture of transparency and trust within the team. When held accountable for their actions, it builds a sense of accountability and encourages everyone to perform their best. It also encourages people to take ownership of their own performance and continuously improve their skills and abilities.

Moreover, when team members work together to share the burden of success or failure, it helps to reduce stress and anxiety. Knowing everyone is working together toward a common goal and that the team is stronger also provides a sense of security. By acknowledging the collective effort and taking personal responsibility, individuals can foster a positive work environment, promote collaboration, and drive success.

ACTION STEPS:

- *Use "we" statements for teamwork:* When working in a team, it's important to use inclusive language acknowledging the collective effort that led to success. Use "we" instead of "me" statements to highlight the team's contributions and achievements. For example, instead of saying, "I did this," say, "We achieved this through our combined effort and hard work."
- *Use "me" statements when taking blame:* It's important to take responsibility for your actions and avoid blaming others when things go wrong. Use "me" instead of "we" statements to take ownership of your mistakes and demonstrate accountability. For example, instead of saying, "We messed up," say, "I made a mistake, and I take full responsibility for it." This not only demonstrates integrity but also helps to avoid damaging trust within the team.
- *Acknowledge individual contributions:* While using "we" statements is important for teamwork, it's also important to acknowledge individual contributions where appropriate.

This can be in private recognition, public acknowledgement, or simply a thank-you. Recognizing individual contributions can boost team morale and encourage people to continue doing their best work.

TEACH OTHERS WHAT YOU CAN

Designation: Knowledge Sharing, Mentorship

LESSON:

You'd be surprised how well people can perform with a knowledge of their craft and room to take action. If you manage adults, treat them as such, not as subordinate children. Be sure to stress the importance of asking questions if necessary so they don't feel pressured to make guesses when they don't know the answer. Learn things on your own as if you will be teaching them later. Doing so will change your perspective and increase your engagement with the thought in mind that you may have to relay the information at a later time.

Passing on your knowledge and wisdom to others can be one of the greatest gifts you can give. It can inspire individuals to pursue their passions, develop their skills, and grow as a result. Those around us can learn and grow by setting an example and demonstrating the right way to perform a task. However, it is important to approach teaching with patience, empathy, and understanding. To effectively teach others, you must understand the learning style of the person you are teaching and provide them with the necessary space and resources to learn. As a teacher, it is also important to balance providing guidance and allowing for independence. While it is essential to set an example and provide instruction, it is equally important to give the individual a chance to take the lead and assume responsibility for their growth and development. When we create an environment where people are free to ask questions, take ownership of their learning, and make mistakes, they can grow into confident and capable individuals.

Moreover, the act of teaching can also be an opportunity for personal growth and development, as you are required to articulate complex ideas in simple terms. When you approach learning with the intent of teaching it later, it can lead to a deeper level of engagement and understanding. It requires you to examine the subject matter from different perspectives and consider how to best convey the information to others. In this way, teaching can be a two-way street, where both the teacher and the student benefit. By imparting what we know to others, we can help shape the future and positively impact the world. It is essential to acknowledge that teaching others what you know is beneficial for those you are teaching and also for yourself. When you teach someone, you examine and refine your own understanding. By being open and generous with your knowledge and skills, you are helping to build a brighter future for yourself, those you teach, and the world.

ACTION STEPS:

- *Teach others what you can when you can:* This can be done as easily as setting an example in any task you're performing or by offering to show someone something if they're willing to learn.
- *Teach others how you would want to be taught:* Be patient, learn their learning style, and ensure there is room to breathe. Do your best not to micromanage. There is a solid line between displaying appropriate work ethic, behaviour,

or how to do something to set an example versus never giving those you teach a chance to take the lead and own some responsibility. We've all worked under micromanagers and possibly micromanaged without noticing it.

- *Identify your strengths:* Identify your areas of expertise and what you can offer to others. Think about your experiences, skills, and knowledge, and consider how you can share them with others.
- *Find opportunities to teach:* This could include volunteering, mentoring, or simply sharing your knowledge with friends, family, or colleagues. Consider offering to teach a class or workshop on a topic you are passionate about.
- *Adapt your teaching style to the needs of your audience:* Consider their learning style, background knowledge, and experience, and adjust your approach accordingly. Be patient and supportive, and encourage questions and discussion.
- *Provide feedback:* Provide feedback to those you are teaching. Offer constructive feedback that helps them grow and improve, and be specific in your feedback. Celebrate their successes and provide guidance in areas where they can improve.
- *Be open to learning:* Teaching others can be a two-way street, and you can learn a lot from the experiences and perspectives of others. Be receptive to feedback and willing to learn and grow with your students.

LEAD FROM THE FRONT

Designation: Leadership, Leading by Example

LESSON:

Lead from the front. As a supervisor or leader in any role you will have your hands full with your own set of tasks and duties, but great leaders are not afraid to take on extra in setting the standard of what they expect. There is no better way to do so than by doing the work they expect of others. Leadership is about setting an example and inspiring others to follow. A great leader understands the importance of leading by example and demonstrates this through their actions and behaviour. When leaders lead from the front, they show their team what it means to work hard, be accountable, and strive for excellence. They are not afraid to roll up their sleeves and do the work they expect of others. This not only sets the standard of what is expected but also builds trust and respect among the team.

Leading from the front is not just about delegating tasks. It also involves taking on additional responsibilities and going above and beyond what is expected of them to get the job done. A leader willing to do the hard work sets a positive tone for the team and shows them that they are committed to their success. Moreover, a leader who leads from the front demonstrates that they are not afraid to get their hands dirty. Leading from the front is about establishing a strong work ethic, setting an example for the team, and showing that you are committed to the success of the organization. It is a key attribute of great leaders and helps to inspire and motivate others to work together to achieve common goals.

ACTION STEPS:

- *Set a positive example:* Leading from the front starts with setting a positive example for others. This means demonstrating the behaviour and values you want to see in others. For example, if you want your team to be collaborative and respectful, make sure you are consistently demonstrating those traits in your interactions with others.
- *Be proactive:* Leading from the front also means being proactive and taking the initiative to drive progress and achieve goals. Don't wait for others to take action or make decisions—be the first to step forward and take responsibility for driving results, which can help inspire and motivate others to follow your lead.
- *Communicate effectively:* Effective communication is critical to leading from the front. Be clear and direct, and ensure your team understands the expectations and goals. Keep the lines of communication open and be willing to listen to feedback and ideas from others. By communicating effectively, you can build trust and inspire others to follow your lead.

COMMON GOALS DESPITE ISSUES

Designation: Teamwork, Perseverance, Problem-Solving, Relationships

LESSON:

The people with whom you surround yourself play a critical role in your success and in attaining your goals. Therefore, you must choose carefully and ensure you have aligned interests with those on your team. This is particularly important in an organizational setting, where the success of the group is dependent upon the cooperation and coordination of all members.

However, it is natural that conflict will arise within any group, regardless of how well its members get along. The key to managing conflict effectively is not letting it impede progress toward the common goal. When disagreements occur, address them directly and calmly and find a way to move forward that takes the perspective of all involved into account. This is also true of relationships. They can be tested by conflict, but it is important to remember that these challenges can strengthen the bond between individuals. If the situation permits, try to rise above the conflict and find a way to work through it together. Doing so will demonstrate your commitment to the relationship and the shared goal of maintaining a positive relationship.

It is important to focus on the bigger picture and keep the ultimate goal you are working toward in mind. By doing so, you will be able to navigate conflicts effectively and continue to make progress toward your common goal, whether in an organizational setting or in your personal relationships.

ACTION STEPS:

- *Clarify the goals:* It's important to clarify and communicate the goals you are trying to achieve. Ensure everyone is on the same page and understands what they are working toward. This can help keep everyone focused and motivated despite any issues or conflicts.
- *Practise active listening:* Listening to others is key to understanding their perspectives and finding common ground. Practise active listening by giving your full attention to others, asking questions to clarify their viewpoints, and

summarizing what you've heard to ensure understanding. This can help build trust and understanding within the group or relationship.
- **Identify and address issues:** If there are issues or conflicts, it's important to address them head-on. Identify the underlying causes and work together to find mutually beneficial solutions. Be open to compromise and find common ground to advance toward the shared goals. Do not lose sight of the goal by getting fixated on the issues.

BUILDING AND MAINTAINING PROFESSIONAL RELATIONSHIPS

Designation: Teamwork, Relationships

LESSON:

Building and maintaining relationships is critical to personal and professional success. The people you meet throughout life can profoundly impact your future by opening doors and creating opportunities you may never have imagined. Strong relationships can help you achieve your goals, personally and professionally. By building a network of supportive and influential individuals, you can gain access to resources and opportunities that might otherwise be unavailable. This is especially true in highly competitive careers or fields where having the right connections can make a huge difference.

Of course, it's important to remember that relationships and professional success are not mutually exclusive. Your work and relationships should complement each other, with each aspect feeding into and reinforcing the other. When you are passionate about your work and committed to your craft, you will be more likely to attract similarly dedicated and motivated individuals. Ultimately, you can find success, fulfilment, and purpose through the relationships you build and the people you meet. So, make an effort to build strong and lasting connections with others, and never underestimate the power of a supportive network to help you achieve your goals and dreams.

ACTION STEPS:

- *Show genuine interest:* One of the most important aspects of building and maintaining relationships is showing genuine interest in others. Take the time to get to know the people in your life, ask questions about their interests and experiences, and actively listen to their responses. This can help build trust and understanding and show others that you value them as individuals.
- *Communicate regularly:* Communication is key to building and maintaining relationships. Whether through phone calls, text messages, or in-person conversations, make sure to communicate with the people in your life regularly. This can help strengthen the bond between you and keep the relationship strong.
- *Be reliable:* This is another important aspect of building and maintaining relationships. Follow through on your commitments, show up on time, and be there for the people in your life when they need you. This can help build trust and show others they can count on you, which is essential for strong and healthy relationships.

DO NOT TAKE GOOD PEOPLE FOR GRANTED

Designation: Relationships, Gratitude

LESSON:

It's all too easy to take good people for granted. Whether it's friends, family, coworkers, or mentors, those who consistently bring positivity and support into our lives can quickly become an afterthought. But the reality is that these individuals play a critical role in our growth, success, and happiness. Good people bring stability, support, and encouragement into our lives. They are there for us when we need them, whether offering a listening ear, providing knowledge or information, lending a shoulder to cry on, or simply sharing a laugh. They help us to keep our focus on our goals and push us to be the best version of ourselves.

More so, good people have a way of challenging us and pushing us to grow. They hold us accountable and help us identify areas we need to improve. This growth is essential to leading a fulfilling life, and good people play an important role in this process.

It's also worth considering that good people are not always easy to come by. True friends, for example, accept us for who we are and support us through thick and thin. Finding such people is no small feat, and when we do, we must hold on to them and appreciate them for the precious gifts they are. Good people can also profoundly impact our lives in ways we may not even be aware of. They bring positivity, light, and joy into our lives and help us to maintain a positive outlook even in the face of adversity. They shape our lives and help us stay on track toward our goals. We mustn't take good people for granted.

ACTION STEPS:

- *Express gratitude:* The first step in not taking good people for granted is to express gratitude for their presence in your life. Take the time to thank them for their contributions and let them know how much you appreciate them. You can do this through a simple thank-you note, a phone call, or even a face-to-face conversation.
- *Show empathy:* Good people often go above and beyond for others, and it's important to show empathy for the challenges they may be facing. Take the time to listen to their concerns and offer support in any way possible. By showing empathy, you demonstrate that you value and care for the person, which can help strengthen the relationship.
- *Invest in the relationship:* Finally, invest in the relationship by actively engaging with the person and taking an interest in their life. Make time for regular conversations, engage in shared activities, and offer support when needed. Investing in the relationship can help you build trust and create a stronger bond that is less likely to be taken for granted. Remember, good people are often hard to come by, and it's important to nurture these relationships to ensure they continue to thrive.

CHECK ON YOUR PEOPLE

Designation: Relationships, Maintaining Positive Professional Relationships

LESSON:

Check on your people. As a leader, you are responsible for ensuring the well-being of those under your charge, especially in times of stress or uncertainty. One way to do this is to debrief after significant events, whether positive or negative. This allows you to check in with your team and get a sense of how they are feeling and coping. If you are not in a leadership position, you may still be able to contribute to the debriefing process by speaking with those involved. This can allow you to offer support, provide feedback, and identify areas for improvement.

In either case, it is important to approach these conversations with empathy and a nonjudgmental attitude. The goal is to foster an open and supportive environment where everyone feels comfortable sharing their experiences and reflections. By proactively checking on your people and conducting debriefs, you demonstrate your commitment to their well-being and help build a stronger and more resilient team. This, in turn, will lead to improved performance and a better outcome for everyone. It is also essential to be proactive in seeking out and addressing any issues that may have arisen during the event. This could include any breakdowns in communication, identifying areas for improvement, and putting measures in place to prevent similar problems from occurring in the future.

It's also important to recognize and acknowledge the efforts and contributions of those involved. This can help boost morale and motivation and foster a sense of pride and accomplishment within the team. It is essential to be honest and transparent in your debriefing process. This means being open about what went well, what didn't go well, and what needs to be done to ensure success in the future. By doing so, you create an environment of trust and accountability, which is essential for building a strong and effective team.

ACTION STEPS:

- *Make time:* One of the most important things you can do to check on your people is to make time for them. This could be a regular check-in, a phone call, or even a quick message to see how they're doing. Make sure to prioritize this time in your schedule and be consistent with it.
- *Listen actively:* When you check on your people, listen actively to their responses. Show genuine interest in their lives, ask open-ended questions, and avoid interrupting or jumping to conclusions. This can help you better understand their needs and concerns and build stronger relationships with them.
- *Offer support:* If your people are going through a tough time, offer your support however you can. This could be as simple as being a listening ear or offering words of encouragement, or it could involve more tangible support like offering to help with a task or providing resources to address a specific need. Let them know that you are there for them and that you care about their well-being.

A STANDARD OF RESPECT

Designation: Respect, Interpersonal Relationships, Communication

LESSON:

Set a standard of respect to give to others unless they give you a reason not to. It is important to remember that respect is not something that must be earned but rather a baseline that you should grant to everyone. This means treating others with dignity, kindness, and compassion, regardless of who they are or their background.

Of course, this does not mean that you should unquestioningly trust or give your loyalty to everyone you encounter. Trust and loyalty are earned through time and consistent behaviour. They require effort, commitment, and a genuine desire to build a strong and meaningful relationship. By setting a high standard for respect and being mindful of whom you trust and give your loyalty to, you can cultivate strong and lasting relationships built on mutual respect, trust, and support. This, in turn, can help you achieve your personal and professional goals and lead to a fulfilling and meaningful life.

ACTION STEPS:

- ***Treat others how you would like to be treated:*** The golden rule of treating others how you would like to be treated is a good standard to follow when giving a neutral standard of respect. This means treating everyone with kindness, compassion, and understanding, regardless of their background, beliefs, or opinions.
- ***Avoid making assumptions:*** To give a neutral standard of respect to everyone, it's important to avoid making assumptions about others. Don't judge people based on their appearance, ethnicity, gender, or any other characteristic. Instead, take the time to get to know them and understand their perspective before making judgments.

"PEOPLE-PLEASING BEHAVIOUR"—INTENTION AND FRAMING

Designation: Interpersonal Relationships, Personal Development

LESSON:

People-pleasing behaviour is not always a bad thing. It's simply knowing how to adapt to environments and being flexible around different personality types. Adapting to different environments and personality types is a key aspect of effective communication and interaction with others. Understanding the motivations, tendencies, and values of those you interact with can go a long way in improving your relationships and achieving your goals. However, it's important to remember that "people-pleasing" behaviour should not come at the cost of compromising your values and beliefs nor losing your sense of self. By remaining grounded in your own principles, you can navigate difficult situations and maintain your sense of integrity, even when dealing with difficult or abrasive personalities.

Additionally, it's essential to understand that everyone has different communication styles, and everyone may not respond well to the same approach. Flexibility and an understanding of different personality types can help you effectively communicate and work with a wide range of individuals but always keep in mind that treating everyone with respect should be the foundation of your interactions. It is possible to maintain your own values and beliefs while still being respectful and courteous toward others. In fact, by staying true to yourself, you can connect with others on a deeper level.

ACTION STEPS:

- *Assess your motives:* Take a look at your reasons for engaging in people-pleasing behaviour. Are you doing it to avoid conflict or to gain approval from others? Or are you doing it because you genuinely enjoy helping others and making effective encounters? If your motives come from a genuine desire to help others, then people-pleasing behaviour can be a positive thing.
- *Set healthy boundaries:* Learn to say no when needed. It's important to prioritize your own needs and well-being and to avoid taking on too much responsibility or sacrificing your happiness to please others.
- *Practise assertiveness:* Communicate your needs and wants clearly and respectfully. This will help you develop healthy relationships based on mutual respect and understanding rather than people-pleasing behaviour.

IF SOMEONE NEAR YOU FALLS, HELP PICK THEM UP

Designation: Compassion, Kindness

LESSON:

If someone near you falls, help pick them up. Whether this is in the literal or figurative sense, the importance of helping those around us cannot be overstated. In fact, it's often said that the measure of a person's character is not how they treat those who can do something for them but how they treat those who can do nothing for them. It's easy to look down on others, to feel superior, or to judge them based on their shortcomings. But it takes real strength of character to see the good in others and to help them rise above their challenges. When someone near us falls, it's easy to look the other way and let someone else deal with the situation. But if we want to positively impact the world around us, we must be willing to step up and lend a hand. It might not always be easy, and it might not always be convenient, but the rewards are immeasurable. Not only do we help others in need, but we also strengthen our sense of purpose and fulfilment.

It's also important to recognize that we all have something to offer, even if it's just a helping hand. We don't need to be wealthy or powerful to make a difference in someone's life. Sometimes, all it takes is a kind word or a small gesture of support. We never know what impact our actions might have, but we can be certain they will be appreciated. So, let us remember to be there for those around us, lift them when they fall, and offer what we can to make the world a better place. We all have the power to make a positive impact, and it's up to us to use that wisely.

ACTION STEPS:

- *Be aware of your surroundings:* To help someone who has fallen, you need to be aware of your surroundings and the people around you. Pay attention to others and look for signs that someone may need help.
- *Approach the situation with empathy:* When you encounter someone who has fallen, approach the situation with empathy and compassion. Put yourself in their shoes and try understanding how they may feel.
- *Offer a helping hand:* If the situation calls for it, offer a helping hand to the fallen person. This may mean physically helping them up if they have fallen or offering emotional support if they are going through a difficult time.

- *Be patient and understanding:* Remember that everyone falls at some point in life, and it is important to be patient and understanding. Offer your support and encouragement, and be there for them as they get back on their feet.
- *Encourage and empower them:* Finally, encourage and empower the fallen person. Help them see the positive aspects of the situation, and offer them the tools and resources they need to get back on track.

It would take lifetimes to gain all the knowledge in the world, but each person you meet possesses a part of it.

III.
PERSONAL DEVELOPMENT

"*Don't wish it were easier, wish you were better. Don't wish for fewer problems, wish for more skills. Don't wish for less challenge, wish for more wisdom.*"

—JIM ROHN

WELCOME TO A NEW CHAPTER ON PERSONAL DEVELOPment—a journey toward unlocking your full potential, achieving your goals, and becoming the best version of yourself. Life is filled with challenges, obstacles, and setbacks that often leave us feeling overwhelmed, stuck, or unfulfilled. However, the power of personal development lies in its ability to transform these challenges into opportunities for growth, resilience, and success.

Personal development is not a one-time event or a quick fix but rather a lifelong journey of continuous improvement and self-awareness. It is about investing in yourself, honing your skills, and developing the mindset to overcome challenges and achieve your dreams. In this chapter, we will explore the principles, strategies, and practical steps to unleash your potential, cultivate resilience, and achieve lasting success. Personal development encompasses various aspects of your life, from your mindset and habits to your relationships and goals. It's about taking ownership of your life, making intentional choices, and continually learning and growing. Through the insights and strategies in this chapter, you will gain a deeper understanding of yourself, your strengths, and your values, which will serve as a solid foundation for your personal and professional growth.

At times, the journey of personal development may be challenging. It requires self-discipline, commitment, and a willingness to step outside your comfort zone. It may require confronting limiting beliefs, overcoming fears, and pushing through obstacles. However, the rewards of personal development are invaluable. It's about building resilience, unlocking your potential, and creating a life aligned with your values and goals.

In the upcoming chapter, we will explore a wide range of topics encompassing personal development, from self-awareness and mindset to goal setting and time management. Each lesson will provide actionable steps to help you apply these principles in your unique situation. The journey of personal development is a continuous process, and the lessons in this book will serve as a roadmap to guide you toward your desired outcomes. As you embark on this chapter on personal development, I urge you to approach it with an open mind, a willingness to learn, and a commitment to taking action. Remember, personal development is not a destination but a lifelong journey toward becoming the best version of yourself. So, get ready to unlock your potential, overcome challenges, and achieve lasting success. The journey continues.

FORWARD THINKING

Designation: Personal Development, Personal Growth

LESSON:

The ability to think ahead is a fundamental aspect of being human. It allows us to anticipate and prepare for the future, set goals and work toward achieving them, and make plans and decisions that will impact our lives. Without forward thinking, we are at the mercy of circumstance and chance, and we may find ourselves unprepared for the challenges that lie ahead. To be a forward thinker, you must be able to visualize and plan for the future, considering various possible outcomes and contingencies. This requires a certain level of imagination, creativity, and strategic thinking. It also requires learning from the past and applying that knowledge to future situations.

One of the most important benefits of forward thinking is that it can help us avoid future problems and conflicts. By anticipating potential challenges and proactively addressing them, we can prevent issues from escalating and avoid unnecessary stress and turmoil. This is especially important in personal relationships, where misunderstandings and miscommunications can often lead to conflict and hurt feelings. Forward thinking is also essential for setting and achieving personal and professional goals. By visualizing what we want to accomplish and working toward those goals methodically and strategically, we can improve our chances of success and create a more fulfilling life. By cultivating this ability and putting it into practise, we can create a more positive and successful future for ourselves and those around us.

ACTION STEPS:

- *Set clear, specific goals:* To think and plan for the future, you need a clear idea of what you want to achieve. Set specific, measurable goals that align with your values and priorities. Make sure your goals are challenging yet achievable, and write them down to increase your commitment.
- *Create a long-term plan:* Once you have set your goals, create a long-term plan that outlines the steps you need to take to achieve them. Break down your plan into smaller, manageable milestones you can focus on achieving one at a time. Your plan should be flexible and adaptable as circumstances change, but it should provide a clear path forward toward your goals.
- *Practise creative problem-solving:* To be forward thinking, you need to anticipate and solve problems before they arise. Practise creative problem-solving techniques, such as brainstorming, mind-mapping, or asking "What if?" questions to help generate new ideas and solutions. By developing your creativity and critical-thinking skills, you can become better at anticipating future challenges and opportunities and responding proactively to them.

OTHERS ADAPTING TO YOUR GROWTH

Designation: Personal Development

LESSON:

Don't be discouraged when people around you don't or can't adapt to your growth. Friends and acquaintances come and go at all stages of life, and if you are on a continuous journey of self-improvement, you will be rising in some areas and falling in areas that may have included things you had in common with others.

As one grows and develops, it is not uncommon for those around them to struggle to keep pace. It is natural for people to change and evolve, but it is common for some to cling to old ways of thinking and acting. When this happens, it is important not to be discouraged or disheartened. Instead, embrace the changes and understand that growth often leads to losing certain relationships and forming new ones. It is important to remember that not everyone can adapt to your growth and improvement. Some may struggle to understand your perspective or new way of thinking, but that does not reflect on your worth or success. On the contrary, it is a sign of your commitment to self-betterment and growth.

Do not be afraid to let go of relationships that no longer serve you or hold you back. As you continue your journey, new and meaningful relationships will develop and grow, providing support and guidance. Focus on the relationships that bring positivity and growth into your life, and do not let the others weigh you down. Remember that self-improvement is a continuous process, and it is not necessary to be at the same stage as others. Embrace the journey, celebrate your successes, and do not let the opinions of others define you. Your journey is your own, and it is up to you to determine what path to take and what relationships to foster.

Don't compromise your beliefs or standards just to fit in or appease others. Be true to yourself, and don't be afraid to stand up for what you believe in. It's important to have a strong sense of self and to know what is essential to you. By doing so, you will attract the right people into your life who will support and uplift you rather than hold you back. Stay open-minded, be willing to learn, and don't hesitate to step outside of your comfort zone.

With persistence, hard work, and a positive attitude, you can continue to progress on your journey toward self-betterment.

ACTION STEPS:

- *Surround yourself with positive and supportive people:* One of the best ways to stay motivated and not get discouraged by others adapting to your growth is to surround yourself with positive and supportive people. Reach out to individuals who encourage you to pursue your goals, believe in your abilities, and are genuinely happy for your success. By surrounding yourself with positivity, you will be more likely to maintain a positive attitude, even in the face of criticism or negativity from others.
- *Reframe negative feedback:* Instead of seeing negative feedback or criticism as a personal attack, try to reframe it as an opportunity to learn and grow. Ask yourself what you can learn from the feedback and how you can use it to improve yourself. Everyone has different perspectives, and sometimes negative feedback can offer valuable insights you might not have considered before.
- *Focus on your own journey:* Comparing yourself to others can be a surefire way to feel discouraged, especially when others seem to be adapting to your growth. Instead, focus on your own journey and celebrate your progress. Set goals for yourself and measure your success based on your progress rather than comparing yourself to others. By focusing on your own journey, you will be less likely to feel discouraged by the success of others.

FUTURE PLANNING

Designation: Personal Development, Self-Improvement

LESSON:

Planning for the future is a critical aspect of success and fulfilment in life. Whether it's in your career, financial situation, or personal life, planning can help you achieve your goals and live the life you desire.

When it comes to your career, having a clear plan in place can help you focus on your strengths, identify growth opportunities, and set achievable goals for the future. This includes clearly understanding your skills and strengths, researching industries and companies that align with your interests and values, and establishing a plan for continuous professional development.

Regarding your financial situation, planning for the future is equally important. This includes creating a budget, saving for emergencies, and investing in your future. It's also essential to clearly understand your long-term financial goals, such as buying a home, starting a family, or retiring comfortably, and developing a plan to achieve them.

In addition to career and financial planning, it's also important to consider preventive measures to prepare for potential challenges in the future. This includes having adequate insurance coverage, developing a comprehensive emergency plan, and taking steps to maintain your physical and mental health.

Planning for the future is not only critical for individual success, but it also demonstrates discipline, focus, and initiative. When you have a plan in place, you are taking control of your life and future and positioning yourself for success. It's important to understand that planning for the future is a continuous process. Your plans and priorities will evolve, and it's crucial to reassess your situation and make adjustments as needed continually. This means being open to new ideas, embracing change, and being proactive in life.

ACTION STEPS:
- *Set clear goals:* Think about what you want to achieve in the short and long term, and write down your goals. By setting goals, you will have a clear target to work toward and a roadmap for achieving them.
- *Make a plan:* Once you have your goals in place, make a plan to achieve them. Break down your long-term goals into smaller, manageable steps that you can take in the short term. Create a timeline and action plan to guide your progress. Regularly review your plan to track your progress and adjust your course as needed.
- *Take action:* Planning is important, but taking action is essential. Once you have your goals and plan in place, move toward achieving your goals. Be proactive, persistent, and flexible in your approach. Remember that setbacks and obstacles are a natural part of the process, and be prepared to adjust your plan as needed. By taking consistent action toward your goals, you will progress and build momentum toward achieving them.

TAKING ACTION WHEN NECESSARY

Designation: Personal Development, Action

LESSON:

If you're stuck and don't know what to do at a certain point, whether on a project or in life, go with something. Anything. Move in any direction, and then you'll better understand whether it is right or wrong. You can always correct as needed and get on the right path. Making a decision can be one of the most difficult things, especially when you are stuck and don't know what to do next. It can be tempting to remain in a state of indecision, waiting for the perfect solution to present itself. However, this approach can often lead to stagnation and a lack of progress.

By taking action, you are setting yourself in motion and creating momentum. This momentum can then be harnessed to help you better understand the situation and find the right path forward. If you find that your initial decision was incorrect, that's okay. You can always correct and adjust your course. The important thing is that you have taken the first step and are now on the path to finding a solution. This approach can be applied to any situation, whether it's a personal problem or a professional project. Whether you are trying to solve a complex problem or simply trying to find your next step, the same principle applies. Just do something. Take action, no matter how small, and start moving in a direction. The more you take action, the more you will learn and the more confident you will become in your ability to make decisions and solve problems. With each step, you will gain the confidence and knowledge to make the right decisions and find the right path forward.

One of the fundamental principles of human existence is

that we are defined by our actions, not by our thoughts or intentions. Ideas are cheap and abundant, but it is the execution of those ideas that separates the successful from the average. By taking action, you are demonstrating your commitment to your goals and values, and you are actively shaping your reality. Taking action is the key to success in both personal and professional endeavours. Don't wait for the perfect solution; don't be afraid to make mistakes, and don't let indecision and procrastination hold you back. Embrace the uncertainty and dare to take action, through which we grow, learn, and find our way to the right path.

ACTION STEPS:

- *Set clear goals:* Setting clear and specific goals can help you identify when action is necessary. Create goals that are measurable, achievable, and time-bound. Divide your goals into smaller steps and create a plan for achieving each step.
- *Prioritize tasks:* When you have multiple tasks to complete, it can be easy to become overwhelmed and unsure where to begin. Prioritizing tasks can help you identify the most important tasks and those that can wait. Make a list of tasks and order them by their level of importance and urgency. Focus on completing the most important tasks first, and use your plan from step one to help you achieve them.
- *Take small steps:* Sometimes, taking action can feel daunting, particularly when the task is large or complex. Taking small steps can help you build momentum and progress toward your goals. Break large tasks into smaller, more manageable steps, and focus on completing one step at a time. Celebrate each small victory and motivate yourself to keep moving forward.

SKILLS WITH LONG-TERM APPLICATIONS AND FINDING COMFORT IN ABSOLUTES

Designation: Personal Development

LESSON:

Pursuing knowledge and self-improvement is a lifelong journey that requires a significant investment of time and energy. However, it is important to focus not just on the amount of information we acquire but also on the quality and relevance of that information. One of the most efficient ways to maximize the return on our investment of time and energy is to seek out skills and knowledge with long-term applications. Such skills are those that can be applied over and over again throughout our lives. You can think of these building blocks as your personal and professional development, and they have the potential to bring you a lifetime of benefits. For example, learning how to manage your finances, communicating effectively, and thinking critically are all skills that have long-term applications and can have a profound impact on our lives.

It can be tempting to focus on short-term goals and immediate gains. Still, the true value of our education and personal development lies in the long-term applications of the skills and knowledge we acquire. To achieve this, you must develop a mindset that values long-term thinking and invests in the long term.

In addition, it is also important to cultivate a mindset of comfort in the absolutes. Certain routine tasks and practises in life are necessary for our well-being and success, such as making your bed, brushing your teeth, and maintaining a healthy diet. These tasks may seem small and insignificant, but they profoundly impact our daily lives. By embracing these absolutes and finding comfort in their routine, we can create a foundation of stability and consistency that supports our personal and professional growth and sets us on a path to success.

ACTION STEPS:
- *Identify transferable skills:* Transferable skills can be applied in multiple contexts and industries. Focus on developing skills with long-term applications that can be useful in different settings. Examples of transferable skills include problem-solving, critical thinking, communication, and leadership. These skills can be valuable no matter what career or field you pursue.
- *Develop a growth mindset:* Having a growth mindset means believing you can develop and improve your skills over time. This mindset can help you embrace challenges and setbacks as opportunities to learn and grow. Rather than seeking comfort in absolutes, focus on the process of learning and improving your skills. This can help you find motivation and satisfaction in the journey rather than just the result.
- *Set realistic and specific goals:* This can help you focus your efforts and develop your skills over time. Rather than seeking quick fixes or absolutes, break down your goals into smaller, achievable steps. Set specific targets for what you want to achieve, and focus on developing the necessary skills. Celebrate your progress along the way, and use it as motivation to keep developing your skills.

FINDING YOUR PROCESS

Designation: Personal Development

LESSON:

Find your process. Determining what motivates us is a crucial aspect of personal growth and development. Our individual motivations drive us toward our goals and aspirations. It is important to understand that everyone deals with things differently, and as a result, what motivates one person may not motivate another. Therefore, identify what drives you and what your triggers are. Initially, many people rely on external triggers for motivation: for example, the desire to impress others, the need to fulfill expectations, or the pursuit of rewards. However, while external triggers can provide short-term motivation, they are often unsustainable in the long term. To truly reach one's full potential and lead a fulfilling life, it's crucial to cultivate internal triggers and have motivation come from within.

Internal triggers come from deep within us and are often more powerful and enduring sources of motivation. For example, having a strong sense of purpose, a deep passion for what you do, or a strong sense of self-esteem and self-worth. Cultivating these internal triggers requires self-reflection, introspection, and a commitment to personal growth. It requires understanding your values, goals, and what truly drives you. By focusing on developing internal triggers, you can ensure your motivation remains consistent and unwavering, even in the face of challenges and setbacks. This is the key to sustained success and a life of fulfilment. By taking the time to understand what motivates you and then converting external triggers to internal ones, you can achieve greatness and reach your full potential.

ACTION STEPS:

- *Identify your goals:* Determine what you want to achieve and what steps you need to take to get there. This will help you identify the process that will work best for you.
- *Experiment with different methods:* Try out different methods and processes to determine what works best. This may involve trial and error, but it is important to keep an open mind and be willing to try new things.
- *Reflect on what works and what doesn't:* After trying different methods, reflect on what works and what doesn't. Consider why specific methods work better for you than others, and what you can do to improve your process.
- *Adapt and refine your process:* Use what you have learned to adapt and refine your process. This may involve making minor or significant changes, depending on what you have discovered about your strengths and weaknesses.
- *Stay flexible:* Remember that your process may need to change over time as you encounter new challenges and opportunities. Stay flexible and open to new ideas and approaches, and be willing to adjust your process as needed to help you achieve your goals.

TAKING AN ACTIVE ROLE IN YOUR ENDEAVOURS

Designation: Personal Development, Self-Improvement, Success Mindset

LESSON:

The concept of balancing patience and active involvement is a critical one, particularly when it comes to our personal and professional endeavours. On one hand, the saying "Good things come to those who wait" is undoubtedly true, as success often requires persistence and the willingness to stick with our goals over the long term. However, simply waiting for success to come to us is not enough. To truly achieve our goals, we must also actively participate in our labors and work toward our desired outcomes. This means taking initiative and being proactive in pursuit of our dreams.

It is important to recognize that instant gratification is a rare and often unsustainable outcome, and that true success often requires hard work and effort. By taking an active role in our endeavours and pursuing our goals with patience and persistence, we can position ourselves for success and achieve the rewards that come with our efforts. Success requires a balance between patience and proactive involvement. By embracing this balance, we can lay the foundation for a fulfilling and rewarding future.

ACTION STEPS:

- *Define your goals:* What do you hope to achieve? What steps will you need to take to get there? Setting clear and specific goals can help you stay focused and motivated, and make it easier to measure your progress along the way.
- *Take ownership of your actions:* Don't wait for others to tell you what to do or how to do it. Instead, be proactive and take initiative. Identify what needs to be done and take action to make it happen.
- *Seek out opportunities for growth:* Seeking opportunities could mean taking on new challenges, seeking feedback and learning from others, or pursuing training or education to develop new skills. By seeking out opportunities for growth and development, you can stay engaged and motivated, and continue to make progress toward your goals.

THE PURSUIT OF EXCELLENCE

Designation: Personal Development, Success Mindset

LESSON:

The pursuit of excellence and the attainment of one's goals are complex endeavours that require not only a steadfast commitment to the chosen path but also a careful balancing of various important aspects of life. You must pay attention to all the key areas of your life and ensure that not one area gets neglected, as neglecting any aspect can jeopardize the delicate balance you have worked hard to establish. This balance may differ from individual to individual and may require different levels of attention at different times, but it is essential for you to maintain it to reach your full potential and achieve your goals. Whether it is career, relationships, family, training, or any other area you choose to focus on in the development of your skills, all of these areas must be given their due attention and effort to see progress.

Commitment and effort toward your goals on a daily basis, even in the smallest amounts, are the key to success. Staying on the course is not only about excelling in your chosen path, but also about giving proper attention to the important aspects of your life. By doing so, you can maintain the balance you need to continue moving forward and eventually achieve the life you desire. Always keep in mind the importance of balance, and never neglect the other important aspects of your life in pursuit of your goals. A proper mindset and a continuous effort, even in the face of challenges, will go a long way in helping you align your interests with your productivity and eventually attain greater benefits in life.

ACTION STEPS:

- *Set high standards for yourself:* Identify what you want to achieve and what success looks like, and set specific and challenging goals that will push you to reach your full potential.
- *Continuously learn and improve:* This might mean seeking out new experiences, taking on new challenges, or pursuing training or education to develop new skills. By seeking out opportunities for growth and development, you can continue to improve and evolve over time.
- *Embrace a growth mindset:* This means believing that your abilities can be developed through hard work, practise, and learning from your mistakes. Rather than fearing failure, view it as an opportunity to learn and grow, and use setbacks as motivation to push harder and continue improving.

STARTING SOMETHING NEW IS NOT ALWAYS EASY, BUT IS OFTEN WORTH IT

Designation: Personal Development

LESSON:

Starting something new is never easy, especially if it's a significant challenge or goal. It's crucial to approach it with careful planning and a thorough understanding of the risks involved. Some individuals may be comfortable with jumping into things headfirst, but for others, it's better to take smaller, more manageable steps. The key is to find what works best for you and take the time to get yourself in the right mindset before launching into your goal. In this way, you can set yourself up for success and avoid becoming overwhelmed or discouraged from the start. By taking the time to prepare and plan, you can build the foundation you need to achieve your goal and overcome any obstacles that may arise along the way.

It's important to remember that slow and steady progress is still progress, and taking small steps is often better than not taking any steps at all. It's okay to start small, as long as you are consistent and focused in your efforts. Building momentum and making steady progress will help you gain confidence and eventually, you may be able to tackle bigger challenges with ease. The key is to stay focused on your goal and never lose sight of it, even when things get tough. One of the biggest obstacles to achieving your goals is the fear of failure. Many people get discouraged when they don't see immediate results and may give up too soon. This is where having a strong sense of discipline and determination can be beneficial. It's important to remember that setbacks are a natural part of the journey, and they should not be seen as failures. Instead, they should be seen as opportunities to learn, grow, and improve.

When it comes to achieving your goals, it's also important to have the right mindset. This means having a positive attitude, being open to new experiences, and being willing to take calculated risks. It's important to have a strong sense of purpose and never give up, no matter what obstacles you face along the way.

ACTION STEPS:

- *Define your goals and purpose:* Before starting something new, take the time to define your goals and purpose clearly. Ask yourself what you want to achieve and why it's important. A clear understanding of your motivations and desired outcomes can help you stay focused and committed when facing challenges.

- ***Develop a plan:*** Once you've defined your goals and purpose, develop a plan to help you achieve them. This might include breaking down your goals into smaller, more manageable steps, identifying potential obstacles and how you'll overcome them, and establishing a timeline for achieving your objectives. By creating a clear plan, you'll be better equipped to take action and make progress toward your goals.
- ***Take action:*** Finally, take action to start something new. This might mean taking a first small step toward your goal, such as conducting research, reaching out to potential partners or collaborators, or learning a new skill. By taking action, you'll build momentum and gain confidence, which can help you stay motivated and make steady progress toward achieving your goals. Remember, starting something new can be challenging, but by taking it one step at a time, you can overcome obstacles and achieve great things.

PEACE IS IN THE PERSPECTIVE OF MIND

Designation: Personal Development, Positive Mindset

LESSON:

There is no bad weather above the clouds. Peace is in the perspective of mind and location. The perspective of one's mind and location plays a critical role in determining peace and happiness. If you believe that the circumstances in your life are bad, then it is natural to feel like you are in the midst of a storm. But if you shift your perspective and focus on the positive aspects of your life, it can be a source of inspiration and motivation. Just as the weather above the clouds is always clear, the same can be true for our lives. By changing our mindset and viewing things positively, we can rise above our difficulties and find peace and happiness.

In the context of self-improvement, this emphasizes the importance of perspective and mindset in determining our level of satisfaction with life. By focusing on our strengths and aligning our goals with them, we can find a sense of purpose and direction. By shifting our mindset to a more optimistic one, we can find peace and happiness in our lives, regardless of the challenges we may face.

ACTION STEPS:

- *Practise mindfulness:* Mindfulness is a powerful tool for finding peace through perspective. By practising mindfulness, you can learn to observe your thoughts and emotions without judgment, which can help you gain a clearer perspective of your situation. Mindfulness techniques, such as meditation, deep breathing, and yoga, can help you develop a calmer and more centered mindset.
- *Reframe your thoughts:* Reframing your thoughts can also help you find peace through perspective. Instead of dwelling on negative thoughts or worries, focus on your situation's positive aspects. Look for opportunities for growth or learning, or try to find gratitude in the present moment. By shifting your perspective in this way, you can reduce stress and find greater peace of mind. Consider the quote from Viktor Frankl in *Man's Search for Meaning*: "Everything can be taken from a man but one thing: the last of the human freedoms—to choose one's attitude in any given set of circumstances, to choose one's own way."
- *Take action:* Finally, taking action can help you find peace through perspective. Sometimes, taking steps to address a

problem or improve your situation can help you feel more in control and reduce stress. Identify small actions you can take to improve your situation and take them one at a time. By taking action and progressing toward your goals, you can find greater peace of mind and a more positive perspective on your situation.

SETTING REALISTIC GOALS

Designation: Personal Development, Growth Mindset

LESSON:

Setting realistic goals for oneself is a crucial aspect of personal growth and self-improvement. Whether in the workplace or at home, setting objectives and striving toward them provides a sense of purpose and direction. It helps individuals maintain focus, work toward a desired outcome, and track their progress.

When it comes to the workplace, it's essential to remember the attributes that made you successful in achieving your job and receiving recognition. Ambition and drive were key elements that helped you reach your goals, and keeping that flame alive is vital. The same applies to all areas of life, whether it be in personal relationships, hobbies, or passions. Keep pushing yourself to achieve more, never settle for mediocrity, and never forget what got you to where you are now.

It is also important to set goals often. Consistently reassessing and setting new objectives ensures that individuals are always pushing themselves forward, continuously growing and learning, and adapting to the ever-changing environment around them. By setting realistic goals and regularly working toward them, individuals can continually progress, develop their skills, and fulfill their potential. Make the most of each day and each opportunity that comes your way.

ACTION STEPS:

- ***Define your goal:*** What do you want to achieve, and what steps do you need to take to get there? Write down your goal and break it into smaller, more manageable steps. (You've seen this one a lot. It's important.)
- ***Assess your resources:*** Assess your available resources to achieve your goal. This could include your time, skills, finances, and support network. Be honest with yourself about what resources you have and what resources you may need to acquire.
- ***Consider potential obstacles:*** Consider what may arise as you work toward your goal. This could include challenges related to your skills, time, finances, or other external factors. By identifying potential obstacles in advance, you can create a plan to address them and keep yourself on track.
- ***Make a plan:*** Lastly, create a plan for achieving your goal that considers your available resources and potential obstacles. Break your goal into smaller, more achievable steps, and set deadlines for each step. Be flexible and willing to adjust your plan as needed, but stay committed to your ultimate goal.

THE IMPORTANCE OF PREPARATION

Designation: Personal Development, Self-Improvement

LESSON:

Proactivity and preparation are large factors in our daily lives, especially when we want to avoid potential problems or difficulties. Being proactive means anticipating potential issues and taking steps to prevent them from happening in the first place. This requires us to think ahead and consider the consequences of our actions, as well as the potential impact they may have on others. To be proactive, it is important to have a well-organized and systematic approach. This includes setting priorities, breaking tasks into smaller and manageable chunks, and developing a plan of action (this has been mentioned quite a few times and will be mentioned a few more times; it's an important part of life). Additionally, being proactive requires staying informed and knowledgeable about the things that matter to us, whether it's a particular task or a specific area of interest.

Moreover, preparation is a key component in the process of being proactive. Preparation involves gathering the necessary resources and information, developing contingency plans, and ensuring that we have the skills and knowledge to carry out our tasks effectively. When we are well prepared, we are better equipped to respond to unforeseen challenges and minimize the impact of any potential problems. Preparation and being proactive are interlinked and essential for success in all aspects of life. By anticipating potential issues, we can take steps to prevent them from happening, thereby ensuring that we are always ready for the challenges that come our way.

ACTION STEPS:

- *Set clear goals:* Start by setting clear goals for what you want to achieve. Identify what you need to prepare for, and be specific about your objectives. This will help you stay focused and motivated, ensuring you are preparing effectively.
- *Develop a plan:* Develop a plan for how you will prepare. Divide your goals into smaller, more manageable steps, and create a timeline for completing each step. This will help you stay organized and ensure that you are making progress toward your goals.
- *Gather information and resources:* Gather the information and resources you need to prepare effectively. This may include research, books, courses, and training materials. Make sure that you have everything you need to succeed and don't be afraid to ask for help or guidance if you need it.
- *Practise:* Practise is an important part of preparation, especially for skills or activities that require physical or mental performance. Practise regularly and set aside time to hone your skills and abilities.

LEARN TO LIFT OTHERS

Designation: Personal Development, Leadership, Teamwork

LESSON:

Learn to lift others. Do not fear that they will grow to outshine you. Embrace it. If you stay on your own path, you will both grow together. It seems to be a deep-seated, intrinsic feeling that everyone has at some point where we want to see others fail. We are all guilty of this at one time or another, and this feeling applies to a range of individuals, from coworkers to friends to family or strangers. If we go on the basis that this feeling comes because deep down we want to do better than them, then there is a healthier alternative. Help others grow, and if you have the feeling of worry that they will become better than you, then use that feeling as a drive to improve yourself beyond what you are teaching.

This feeling of wanting to see others fail can be a hindrance to our personal and professional growth. It can limit our ability to form meaningful connections and relationships, and also hinder our potential for growth and development. Instead, it is important to adopt a mindset of lifting others, where we strive to help and support those around us in their personal and professional growth. By doing so, we not only foster a sense of community and collaboration, but we also challenge ourselves to continually improve and strive for excellence.

This idea of lifting others is not about being passive or relinquishing control. It is about taking the initiative to help others grow and develop and doing so in a way that empowers them to reach their full potential. By embracing this mindset, we can create a supportive environment where everyone is encouraged to grow and reach their goals, regardless of whether they may outshine us in the future. Additionally, by focusing on our own growth and development, we can stay on our own path and continue to improve ourselves. This way, we can grow alongside those we are lifting, creating a symbiotic relationship that benefits both parties. By lifting others, we also set a positive example and demonstrate our commitment to excellence and growth, which creates a ripple effect that can positively impact our community and the world at large.

ACTION STEPS:

- *Develop empathy:* Put yourself in others' shoes and try to understand their perspectives. This will help you to better relate to them and understand their needs and challenges.
- *Build relationships:* Take the time to get to know others and show genuine interest in their lives. Listen actively, ask questions, and provide support when needed. This will help you to build trust and rapport with others and create a positive and supportive environment.
- *Provide encouragement:* Recognize the strengths and accomplishments of others, and provide positive feedback and support. Celebrate their successes and help them to overcome any obstacles they may face. By providing encouragement, you can help to build confidence and motivation in others.
- *Share knowledge and skills:* Provide mentorship, coaching, or training. Help others to develop their skills and reach their potential by sharing your expertise and providing guidance and support.
- *Be a role model:* Demonstrate positive values and behaviours. Lead by example and inspire others to be their best selves.

THE IMPORTANCE OF ROUTINE

Designation: Personal Development, Self-Improvement

LESSON:

Having a routine provides structure and stability in life. It allows individuals to have a clear sense of direction and purpose, reducing the feeling of confusion and aimlessness. Routine can bring a sense of comfort and predictability, creating a sense of security in the face of uncertainty and chaos. It is also important to understand that a routine should not be rigid and inflexible. It is essential to refresh and modify the routine as needed to prevent boredom and stagnation. Adapting and changing is key in life, and the same principle applies to routine. By embracing change and being open to adjusting routines as needed, individuals can continue to grow and evolve, achieving greater success and fulfilment.

Additionally, recognize the importance of having a balance between routine and spontaneity. While routine provides a sense of stability and structure, it is equally important to have the freedom to break away from routine and embrace new experiences and opportunities, leading to a fulfilling and well-rounded life.

ACTION STEPS:

- *Assess your current routine:* Look at your current routine and assess whether it is serving you well. Identify areas where you may be wasting time or being less productive than desirable, as well as the times you feel stressed or overwhelmed. This will help you to identify areas where you can make improvements.
- *Create a new routine:* This may mean setting a regular sleep schedule, creating a morning routine, or scheduling specific times for exercise or self-care. Be sure to include both productive and leisure activities, and give yourself some flexibility to adjust as needed.
- *Stick to your routine:* Sticking to your routine is key to making it a habit. Set reminders or use a calendar to help you stay on track and make adjustments as needed. Remember that it takes time to develop a new habit, so be patient and consistent in your efforts.

TAKING LESSONS FROM EVERYTHING

Designation: Personal Development, Growth

LESSON:

Learning is a never-ending journey, and every experience, interaction, and encounter in our lives has the potential to be a valuable lesson. We can choose to look at them with an open mind, reflect, and consider what could have gone better or worse, and examine what we can do differently in the future. To cultivate a habit of taking a lesson from everything, we must embrace the principle of openness—to new ideas, new perspectives, and new ways of thinking. When we approach life with a curious mind, we free ourselves from the lessons the world has to offer. We learn to grow from the challenges and triumphs that come our way rather than being defeated by them.

But remember, learning from experiences requires more than just openness. It requires effort. We must take the time to reflect on our experiences, understand the lessons they hold, and apply them to our lives. This requires a level of discipline and dedication that can be challenging, but the reward is well worth it. By embracing openness and dedicating ourselves to reflection and learning, we can make the most of every experience in our lives.

ACTION STEPS:

- *Practise mindfulness:* This is key to learning from every experience. Be present in the moment and observe your surroundings and your thoughts without judgment. This will help you to develop a greater awareness of your surroundings and your own reactions to them. The easiest (although not always pleasant) lessons to learn are the ones that arise from reflecting on your own or others' successes or from failures.

- *Reflect on your experiences, both positive and negative:* Think about what you learned from each experience, and how you can apply those lessons to your future actions and decisions. Reflecting on your experiences can also help you identify patterns and areas for growth.
- *Cultivate a growth mindset:* Embrace challenges as opportunities to learn and grow. Rather than seeing failures or setbacks as a negative experience, view them as an opportunity to learn and improve. This mindset can help you to approach every experience with a positive and open attitude.
- *Keep a journal:* Finally, consider keeping a journal to document your experiences and reflect on what you have learned. This can help you develop a deeper understanding of yourself and your experiences and to track your progress as you continue to learn and grow.

BEING OPEN TO CHANGE

Designation: Personal Development, Growth

LESSON:

Change is a constant in life, and sometimes it can be difficult to admit when we are wrong or need to make adjustments to our perspectives or actions. However, it is important to recognize that growth and learning can happen at any point in our lives. Embracing the willingness to change is a sign of strength and maturity. It demonstrates that you are willing to consider new information and adjust your beliefs and behaviours accordingly.

When you embrace change, you also open yourself up to new opportunities and growth.

Of course, some people may criticize or question your change, but it is important to stand firm in your beliefs and communicate why you are making the change. Explain that you have learned new information or had a change of perspective and that it is important for you to align your actions with your values. Doing so shows that you are confident in your decisions and that you have the courage to take ownership of your choices.

Remember, change is not always easy, but it is always possible. Embrace the opportunity to grow and become the best version of yourself, no matter your stage of life. It's important to understand that growth and evolution are natural processes. Never be afraid to make a change for the better. Don't let the fear of being judged or criticized hold you back from improving yourself and your actions. Instead, embrace the opportunity to make positive changes in your life, and always strive for self-improvement. Remember, everyone makes mistakes and has room for growth. The key is to learn from those mistakes, embrace change, and continue to strive for excellence in all aspects of life.

ACTION STEPS:

- *Embrace discomfort:* Change often involves stepping outside of your comfort zone. Instead of resisting discomfort, embrace it as an opportunity to grow and learn. Challenge yourself to try new things, even if they make you feel uncomfortable or uncertain.
- *Practise mindfulness:* Being present and mindful can help you stay open to change. Take time each day to meditate,

journal, or simply reflect on your thoughts and emotions. This can help you stay grounded and centered, even in the face of change. (You've seen this one quite a bit also. It's important.)
- *Focus on the benefits:* Change can be scary, but it often brings new opportunities and experiences. Instead of focusing on the potential risks or downsides, focus on the benefits that change can bring. This can help you stay motivated and positive, even when facing uncertainty.

TRUST YOUR INSTINCTS

Designation: Self-Awareness

LESSON:

Trust your instincts. Learn to listen to that "gut" feeling. Have you ever gone into a situation that ended badly, and you recall feeling unease before entering that situation? Trusting your instincts can often be the difference between a positive and negative outcome. Our instincts are a combination of our experiences, emotions, and observations. They serve as a warning system, telling us when something is wrong or off. The key to trusting your instincts is to pay attention to them and take them seriously.

When faced with a situation where your instincts tell you to proceed with caution, it's important to listen. This means taking the time to assess the situation, consider the risks and rewards, and then decide based on that information. Trusting your instincts does not mean blindly jumping into a situation without considering the consequences. Instead, it means making informed decisions that consider your intuition and inner voice. Sometimes, our instincts may not be completely accurate, but that doesn't mean you should ignore them. Our instincts are often rooted in a deep knowledge of ourselves and what we need to be safe and successful. You should still respect them even when they may not be right in a specific situation. When we trust our instincts, we can respond quickly and effectively to a situation, rather than hesitating or getting caught off guard. By being aware of this, you can make more informed decisions, respond more quickly to potential threats, and create a better future for yourself.

ACTION STEPS:

- *Be present in the moment:* By tuning in to your thoughts and feelings, you can become more aware of your instincts and intuition. Regularly practising this can help you become more attuned to your inner voice and more confident in following your instincts.
- *Test your instincts:* Another way to start trusting your instincts is to test them in low-stakes situations. For example, if you have a hunch that a certain path is right, try following it and see what happens. As you gain more experience following your instincts, you'll start to build confidence in your ability to trust your inner voice.
- *Reflect on your past experiences:* Take some time to reflect on past experiences when you followed your instincts and it worked out well. What did it feel like when you followed your gut, and what was the outcome? Reflecting on these experiences can help you build confidence in your ability to trust your instincts in the future. If you had an experience where you ignored your instincts and it led to a negative outcome, reflect on what you could have done differently and use that knowledge to inform your future decision-making.

TRY NEW OPPORTUNITIES

Designation: Personal Growth, Exploration

LESSON:

Try out opportunities that arise and test them if you're curious. Opportunities often result from hard work and dedication, but also require a willingness to take risks and step outside of your comfort zone. When an opportunity arises that piques your curiosity, it's important to seize it and see where it takes you. If you're curious about a new opportunity, don't hesitate to test it. The worst that can happen is you may learn that it's not what you expected. On the other hand, you may also discover something new and valuable that expands your knowledge and skillset.

It's important to approach new opportunities with an open mind and a willingness to learn. Don't be afraid to ask questions, seek feedback, and try new things. The more you experiment and explore, the more you grow and develop. Taking chances and trying new things is key to personal growth and development. By embracing opportunities and stepping outside your comfort zone, you'll develop resilience and a growth mindset that will serve you well in all areas of your life.

Taking on new opportunities also helps build your confidence and self-esteem. As you tackle new challenges and succeed, you'll develop a sense of pride and self-assuredness that will carry over into other areas of your life. Remember, you should approach new opportunities with a sense of purpose and direction. Set clear goals and have a plan in place to achieve them. This will help you stay focused and motivated as you navigate new experiences.

You should be prepared, however, to face failures and setbacks along the way. These are an inevitable part of the learning process, and they can provide valuable lessons that help you grow and improve. Don't let failure discourage you; instead, view it as an opportunity to learn and do better next time. By embracing new experiences and taking risks, you'll expand your knowledge, develop new skills, and grow as a person. So, don't be afraid to take that leap and see where it takes you.

ACTION STEPS:

- *Step out of your comfort zone:* Trying new opportunities often means stepping out of your comfort zone. To do this, you need to be willing to take risks and try new things, even if they make you feel uncomfortable or uncertain. One way to ease into this is to start with small steps. For example, if you're nervous about public speaking, try volunteering to speak in front of a small group of friends or colleagues. As you gain confidence and experience, you can gradually take on more significant challenges.
- *Embrace failure:* Trying new opportunities often means facing the possibility of failure. It's important to remember that failure is a natural part of the learning process. Embrace the idea that it's okay to make mistakes and failure can be a valuable teacher. Instead of seeing failure as a setback, use it as a form of feedback and an opportunity to learn and grow.
- *Set clear goals:* Doing so can help you stay focused and motivated as you try new opportunities. When setting goals, be specific about what you want to achieve and when. This will give you a sense of direction and purpose and help you stay on track when things get tough. Additionally, setting goals can help you measure your progress and celebrate your successes along the way.

CALCULATED RISKS

Designation: Personal Growth, Professional Growth

LESSON:

If you want to get ahead in life, you must be willing to take calculated risks. Taking calculated risks means making informed decisions based on research, analysis, and a clear understanding of the potential outcomes. By taking calculated risks, you can push beyond your comfort zone and tackle new challenges that have the potential to bring you closer to your goals. It's important to remember that risks come in many shapes and sizes and can be tailored to your strengths, interests, and aspirations.

When taking calculated risks, it's crucial to clearly understand your objectives and the steps you need to take to achieve them. This includes having a solid plan in place, identifying potential risks, and developing strategies to mitigate them, as well as being prepared to adapt as the situation evolves.

Additionally, this requires a certain level of self-awareness and the ability to manage your emotions. This means having the confidence to trust in your instincts and make decisions that align with your values and beliefs. By embracing opportunities, staying focused on your goals, and having the courage to step outside of your comfort zone, you'll develop the skills and experience needed to achieve greatness. Take that first step, trust in yourself, and watch your life unfold in exciting and meaningful ways.

ACTION STEPS:
- *Do your research:* Before taking a risk, it's important to do your research and gather as much information as pos-

sible. This includes understanding the potential benefits and drawbacks of the opportunity, as well as the potential consequences of both success and failure. By doing your research, you can make an informed decision about whether or not to take the risk.

- *Consider the worst-case scenario:* When taking a calculated risk, it's important to consider the worst-case scenario. What happens if things don't go as planned? Are you prepared to handle the consequences? By considering the worst-case scenario, you can prepare for potential setbacks and make a more informed decision about whether or not to take the risk.
- *Start small:* Taking calculated risks doesn't have to mean making big, bold moves all at once. In fact, it's often better to start small and build up gradually. For example, if you're thinking about starting your own business, you could start by doing some freelance work on the side to test the waters. As you gain more experience and confidence, you can gradually take on bigger risks. This approach can help you develop the skills and knowledge you need to make informed decisions about bigger risks in the future.

SUCCESS IS AN ONGOING JOURNEY

Designation: Personal Growth, Motivation

LESSON:

Success is not a final destination; it's an ongoing journey. Those who attain it must continuously work to maintain and improve it. The moment we become complacent is the moment we start to slide backward. It is important to remember that we must always strive to earn what we have rather than take it for granted. The notion of earning one's way is not limited to material possessions or financial success; it also applies to personal growth, relationships, and overall well-being. Earning your way means embracing challenges and pushing yourself out of your comfort zone. It means taking responsibility for your life—both the successes and failures. When faced with obstacles, you must be determined to overcome them, not by giving up, but by persevering through them. This mindset creates a cycle of success that is self-reinforcing.

To maintain success, it is important to regularly reflect on where you stand and what you have accomplished. This introspection allows you to take stock of progress and identify areas you need to improve. It also provides the opportunity to celebrate achievements and appreciate the work that went into earning them. However, the focus must always remain on the future and what you can do to continually earn your way in life. Whether it's through personal growth, learning new skills, or working hard to achieve a goal, the key is to never stop striving.

ACTION STEPS:

- *Embrace growth and learning:* Success is not a destination but a journey that requires continuous growth and learning. Embrace the mindset of a lifelong learner and be open to new experiences and opportunities to improve your skills and knowledge. Seek feedback and constructive criticism from others, and use this to help you grow and improve.
- *Celebrate small wins:* While keeping your sights set on long-term goals is important, it's equally important to celebrate small wins along the way. Recognize and celebrate your achievements and milestones, no matter how small they

may seem. This can help you maintain motivation and build momentum toward your larger goals.
- ***Reframe failures as learning opportunities:*** It's inevitable that you will encounter setbacks and failures on the road to success. Rather than seeing these as roadblocks, reframe them as opportunities to learn and grow. Ask yourself what you can discover from each experience and how you can use this to improve your skills in the future. Doing so allows you to turn failures into valuable learning experiences while maintaining a growth mindset.

ASKING FOR HELP

Designation: Personal Growth, Self-Improvement, Humility

LESSON:

Don't be afraid to ask for help where needed. Many people are excited at the thought of helping someone with a problem. Whether in your work or personal life, go to those in your circle that you can rely on if need be. Nobody is perfect, and not one person is great at everything. Creating a team of minds will prevail any day. Asking for help is a sign of strength, not weakness. It takes courage to admit that you need assistance and are willing to seek it out. In doing so, you demonstrate your ability to understand your limitations and seek the support of others. This is a critical aspect of developing a strong and supportive community in which individuals can work together and support one another in their respective endeavours.

When seeking help, it is important to approach those you trust and respect. They are the best people who can offer you the support you need, whether that involves seeking advice, guidance, or simply someone in whom to confide. Whatever the situation may be, having someone to turn to can help ease the burden of whatever challenges you are facing and help you move forward confidently. It is also important to remember that seeking help is a two-way street. By opening up to others and offering your support and expertise, you can create a strong and supportive network of individuals who are there for one another. This network can provide the resources you need to overcome obstacles, reach your goals, and live a fulfilling and meaningful life.

ACTION STEPS:
- *Recognize the benefits of asking for help:* This can include getting the support and resources you need to achieve your goals, learning from others with more experience or knowledge, and building stronger relationships with those around you. When you view asking for help as a positive and productive behaviour, it can become easier to do when needed.
- *Identify potential sources of support:* To make it easier to ask for help, it's important to identify potential sources of support in advance. This can include trusted friends or family members, mentors, coaches, or colleagues. Make a list of the people you trust and respect in your life, who may be able to provide support or resources when needed. This can help you feel more confident about asking for help and make it easier to reach out when needed.
- *Be specific and clear about your needs:* When asking for help, be specific and clear about your needs. This can help others understand exactly what you need and make it easier for them to provide the support or resources you require. Be honest and direct about your situation, and tell the person

how they can help. This can help create a more effective and efficient process for getting the help you need and reduce the likelihood of misunderstandings or miscommunications. Remember, everyone needs help at some point, and asking for it is a sign of strength, not weakness.

AWARENESS OF MORTALITY

Designation: Personal Growth, Mindfulness, Existentialism

LESSON:

Awareness of our mortality is a powerful motivator, and by keeping death at the forefront of our thoughts, we can cultivate a sense of urgency and purpose in our lives. Days that have passed are gone forever, and the days to come are finite and limited. This realization can inspire us to make the most of the time that we have and to avoid wasting opportunities and precious moments. It is important to remain passionate about our goals and to continue making progress, even when faced with challenges and obstacles.

While taking breaks and recharging is important, keeping productivity and growth at the front of our minds is crucial. The reality is that we only get one life, and our time on this earth is limited. This means that it is essential to weigh different areas of our lives, focus on what truly matters, and identify what does and does not fit our goals and values.

The legacy we leave behind is an important consideration, and it is essential to consider what kind of impact we want to have on the world and those around us. By embracing a sense of urgency and a growth-oriented mindset, we can make the most of our time on earth and create a legacy we can be proud of.

Keeping death in mind is also a way to cultivate gratitude and appreciation for life. When we acknowledge the fragility and brevity of existence, it can help us to see each day as a gift and cherish our moments. It is also a way to maintain perspective and avoid getting bogged down by the small, petty concerns that can distract us from the things that truly matter. By embracing a sense of mortality, we can focus on what is important and avoid being sidetracked by trivialities. Furthermore, it is important to remember that our legacy is not just about what we leave behind when we die but also about our impact on others while we are alive. Thus, we can inspire others and encourage them to make the most of their time on earth.

In this way, keeping death in mind can be a powerful motivator, a way to cultivate gratitude and appreciation, and a tool for helping us to stay focused on what truly matters. By embracing this awareness, we can create a rich and meaningful life and leave a legacy we can be proud of.

ACTION STEPS:
- *Reflect on your life and priorities:* Think about what matters most to you and what you want to achieve in the time you have left. This can help you gain perspective and focus on what's truly important.
- *Live in the present moment:* Being aware of your mortality can help you appreciate the present moment and make the most of each day. Stay mindful and present in your daily activities rather than dwelling on the past or worrying about the future. Make time for the people and activities you love, and savour the moments you have.
- *Plan for the future:* While it's important to live in the present moment, it's also important to plan for the future in the

event of a worst-case scenario. This might mean creating a will, planning your estate, or discussing end-of-life wishes with your loved ones. Having a plan in place can help you feel more in control and at peace with your mortality and ensure that your wishes are respected.

EXPLORING INTERESTS

Designation: Personal Growth, Self-Discovery

LESSON:

Exploration and experimentation are essential components of personal and professional growth. Whether you're just starting on your career journey or seeking a change after many years in a particular field, it is important to be open to new experiences and opportunities.

One of the challenges of exploring different avenues of interest is balancing the desire to pursue your passions with the need to make a living. While it may be tempting to follow your heart and ignore financial considerations, it is important to be mindful of the practical realities of making a living. You must be able to support yourself and your loved ones, so you must be mindful of the financial implications of your choices.

However, it is equally important to remember that life is short (more so from a career longevity standpoint), and you only get one chance to live. You don't want to look back on your life with regret, wishing you had taken a different path or pursued other interests. By embracing new experiences and exploring different avenues of interest, you can grow as a person and discover new passions that can bring meaning and purpose to your life. So don't be afraid to take risks, step out of your comfort zone, and explore new paths. By doing so, you can find fulfilment and satisfaction in your life and make the most of your time.

ACTION STEPS:
- *Make a list:* Start by listing things you are interested in exploring. This could be anything from trying a new hobby to exploring a new career path. Write down as many things as possible, even if they seem far-fetched or unrealistic.
- *Try new things:* Once you have a list of potential interests, try them out. Sign up for a class, join a club, or simply set aside some time to explore independently. The key is to be open to new experiences and not be afraid to step outside your comfort zone.
- *Reflect on your experiences:* After trying out new things, take some time to reflect on your experiences. What did you enjoy about the experience? What didn't you like? Did you learn anything new about yourself or the world around you? This reflection can help you identify what interests you and guide your future explorations.
- *Repeat the process:* Don't be afraid to repeat this process multiple times; try out new things and reflect on your experiences. This can help you refine your interests and find new ones you may not have thought of before.

GIVING YOURSELF A CHANCE

Designation: Personal Growth, Self-Improvement, Self-Belief

LESSON:

When it comes to wellness, you must give yourself a chance. Maintaining good health and wellness is a crucial aspect of a fulfilling life, and it all starts with taking care of yourself. If you're feeling down or unmotivated, it can be difficult to find the energy and drive to take action, but you must do so.

One effective way to overcome this lack of motivation is to adopt a "fake it until you make it" approach. By taking small, meaningful steps toward your goals, even when you're not feeling particularly motivated, you can begin to build momentum and gain confidence.

For example, if you're feeling down and unmotivated, you might start with something that gets you active like going for a walk, a workout, or tackling a project you've been putting off. By taking these small steps, you can build momentum and feel better about yourself. And when you finally complete these tasks, you'll find that you didn't just fake it; you made it with concrete proof. In this way, you can build up the habits and behaviours necessary for maintaining good health and wellness and gradually begin to see real improvement in your physical and mental well-being. By taking care of yourself and giving yourself the chance to succeed, you can lead a more fulfilling and meaningful life.

ACTION STEPS:
- *Practise self-compassion:* This means treating yourself with kindness, understanding, and forgiveness. Don't beat your-

self up over mistakes or failures. Instead, focus on what you can learn from them and how to move forward. Be kind to yourself and give yourself the same support and encouragement you would give a friend.

- *Take action:* The most important step in giving yourself a chance is taking action. Start taking small steps toward your goals, even if they are scary or uncomfortable. Don't let fear or self-doubt stop you from pursuing what you truly want. Remember, taking action is the only way to create change and progress toward your goals.
- *Seek support:* It's important to seek support from others when giving yourself a chance. Surround yourself with people who believe in you and encourage you to pursue your dreams. Don't be afraid to ask for help when needed, and remember you don't have to do everything alone.

ADMITTING MISTAKES

Designation: Personal Growth, Accountability, Honesty

LESSON:

When it comes to mistakes, by admitting your error right away, people will gain respect for you. If you've had a moment to process it and come up with a solution to the problem, they will respect you even more and, in turn, will be more trusting of you to come forward to them with problems. Not all leaders are conscious enough to think this way, however. Some may see an employee approach them with a problem, and they strictly focus on that problem without acknowledging the employee's forward attitude. This can be annoying, but despite this, it will often be better to come forward and admit an error right away.

Admitting ignorance or mistakes is a sign of maturity and strength rather than a weakness. This type of humility fosters a sense of respect among those who interact with you, demonstrating that you are honest and self-aware. When you admit to not knowing something, you avoid getting involved in a debate or conversation you are not equipped to handle, thus preventing unwanted arguments and misunderstandings. The same goes for when you make a mistake. By admitting to it, you are taking responsibility for your actions, showing that you are accountable and trustworthy. People are more likely to have confidence in your abilities when you are transparent about your limitations and mistakes, as it shows that you have nothing to hide. This can create a culture of open communication, where people feel comfortable coming to you with their own problems and challenges.

However, it's important to remember that not all leaders are attuned to this type of openness. Some may prioritize resolving the problem over acknowledging the employee's proactive approach. Despite this, it's still best to come forward and admit your error as soon as possible, as it can lead to better problem-solving and build stronger relationships in the long run.

ACTION STEPS:

- *Take responsibility:* When you make a mistake, take ownership of it. Avoid blaming others or making excuses, and acknowledge that you made an error. This shows you are willing to take responsibility for your actions and helps build trust with others. How many of us have seen movies where it could've ended in ten minutes if the protagonist had admitted to his error instead of turning it into a debacle that made us feel a great sense of third-party awkwardness?

- *Apologize:* Apologize for your mistake and any harm it may have caused. Offer a sincere apology and take steps to make things right if possible. This demonstrates that you care about the impact of your actions on others and are committed to making things right. Additionally, you'd be surprised how many people will respect you for not getting involved in a debate or conversation you know nothing about or not enough to speak about it. You can simply say, "Hey, I don't know enough about that subject to have an opinion on it." This can prevent many unwanted arguments, debates, or lines of questioning relating to something you know nothing about.
- *Learn from your mistake:* Reflect on what went wrong and what you can do differently in the future. Use your mistake as a learning opportunity to grow and improve. By learning from your mistakes, you can avoid making similar errors in the future and continue to develop as a person.
- *Move forward:* Once you have acknowledged your mistake, apologized, and learned from it, it's important to move forward. Avoid dwelling on the mistake or beating yourself up over it. Instead, focus on what you can do differently in the future and continue to work toward your goals.

THE PURSUIT OF KNOWLEDGE

Designation: Personal Development, Growth

LESSON:

The pursuit of knowledge is an ongoing process, and it's essential to remain open to learning from a diverse range of sources. We must not limit ourselves to only one method of acquiring knowledge, which can lead to boredom and stagnation. Instead, we should embrace multiple sources of information, constantly exploring new and different ways to expand our understanding of the world.

By switching up our learning methods, we can keep our minds engaged and maintain a fresh perspective. For example, suppose you've been reading books on a particular subject. In that case, you may find that listening to audiobooks or podcasts can offer a new and refreshing take on the same material. Similarly, engaging in verbal discussions with others can provide valuable insights and broaden our knowledge base in ways other methods may not. It's important to approach learning with an open mind and a willingness to explore new avenues. Only by embracing diverse knowledge sources can we continue to grow and develop as individuals. Whether through reading, listening, speaking, or any other method, the key is to remain committed to expanding our understanding and never becoming complacent in our quest for knowledge.

ACTION STEPS:

- *Cultivate a love of learning:* Seek out knowledge and information regularly. Read books, attend lectures, take courses, or engage in discussions with others who share your interests. Make learning a habit and a part of your daily routine.
- *Set specific learning goals:* Set specific learning goals for yourself and work toward them consistently. This could include acquiring a new skill, gaining knowledge in a particular subject area, or developing expertise in a specific field. Break down your goals into smaller, more manageable steps, and track your progress.
- *Embrace challenges:* See them as opportunities for growth

and learning. Don't be afraid to take on new challenges, even outside your comfort zone. Push yourself to learn new things and take on new experiences that challenge you and help you grow.
- *Seek out diverse perspectives:* Seek out diverse perspectives and opinions on the subjects that interest you. This will help you broaden your understanding and gain new insights into the world. Seek viewpoints that challenge your assumptions and beliefs, and be open to learning from others.
- *Stay curious:* Finally, stay curious and never stop asking questions. Pursuing knowledge is a lifelong journey, and there is always more to learn and discover. Stay curious and keep an open mind, and you will continue to grow and learn throughout your life.

DISCOVER YOUR LEARNING STYLE

Designation: Personal Growth, Self-Awareness

LESSON:

Learning is a crucial aspect of personal and professional growth. It is a lifelong journey, and it is essential to discover the most effective methods of acquiring and retaining information. While some may argue that various learning styles are more suited for specific age groups, such as children being visual learners, it's crucial to remember that everyone is unique, and the best way to learn is the one that works best for you.

Determining your preferred learning style is one of the first steps in maximizing your learning potential. Some individuals may be visual learners and retain information best through images, while others may learn better through auditory means, such as lectures or discussions. Others may prefer hands-on learning or a combination of multiple styles.

Once you have determined your preferred learning style, you can tailor your education and professional development efforts to best suit your needs. For example, if you are a visual learner, you may find that watching instructional videos or reading illustrated books helps you better understand a concept. If you're an auditory learner, attending lectures or participating in discussions may be more beneficial.

No matter your learning style, the key is to remain open to new methods of learning and continually seek new and innovative ways to improve your education. Whether it's through reading, attending workshops, or taking online courses, there are countless opportunities to expand your knowledge and refine your learning style. As Jim Kwik said in his book *Limitless*, "If knowledge is power, learning is your superpower." With a focus on finding the best learning style for you, you can unleash your full potential and achieve greater success in all areas of your life.

ACTIONS STEPS:

- *Identify your learning style:* There are many different learning style models, including visual, auditory, and kinesthetic. Take a learning style assessment to help you identify your preferred learning style.
- *Experiment with different study techniques:* Once you have identified your learning style, try different study techniques tailored to your style. For example, if you are a visual learner, you might use diagrams, charts, and graphic organizers to help you learn.
- *Reflect on what works:* After trying different study tech-

niques, reflect on what works for you. Think about which techniques help you learn best and why.

- *Incorporate your preferred techniques into your learning process:* Use what you have learned about your learning style to incorporate your preferred study techniques into your learning process. This may involve adapting your approach to studying, changing how you take notes, or finding new resources to support your learning.
- *Continuously assess and adjust:* Remember that learning is a dynamic process, and your learning style and study techniques may change over time. Continuously assess your progress and adjust your approach to learning as needed to ensure you are making the most of your strengths and preferences.

THE FEAR OF FAILURE AS A MOTIVATOR

Designation: Personal Growth, Self-Improvement

LESSON:

Fear of failure is not something to be ashamed of. On the contrary, it is a powerful motivator that can drive us to success. Acknowledging the possibility of failure can be the spark that ignites the fire of our desires and pushes us to learn, adapt, and overcome adversity. The stress that comes with the fear of failure, known as eustress, can be a beneficial force, allowing us to focus and achieve more in a shorter period of time than we would if we had more time to complete a task. When we are under pressure, we have no choice but to be our best. Our minds are sharp, our focus is unwavering, and our drive is unyielding. It is in these moments that we are most productive, most creative, and most capable. Embrace the fear of failure and use it to your advantage. Let it motivate you to improve, push yourself to your limits, and reach for the stars.

In the end, it is not the fear of failure that holds us back, but our doubts, insecurities, and limitations. Let go of those things that hold you back and embrace the fear of failure as a driving force to achieve greatness. Instead of being afraid of the possibility of failure, embrace it and use it to your advantage. Recognize that failure is a natural part of growth and learning, and it can provide valuable lessons and experiences that will help you improve in the future. The mere fact that you are aware of the possibility of failure means that you are already ahead of the curve, as many people are too afraid to even consider the possibility of failure, and thus never challenge themselves to grow and improve. With hard work, dedication, and a willingness to learn from your mistakes, you can overcome any obstacle that stands in your way and achieve great success in life.

ACTION STEPS:

- *Set realistic goals:* Set achievable yet challenging goals. By attaining goals, you can build confidence and momentum. However, it's also important to set goals that push you outside your comfort zone and allow for growth.
- *Take action:* Start moving, even if it means making mistakes or experiencing setbacks. It's important to keep forward momentum rather than getting stuck in fear or self-doubt.
- *Practise self-compassion:* Be kind to yourself. Recognize that everyone experiences failure at some point and that it's a natural part of the learning process.
- *Reframe failure:* Lastly, reframe your perspective on failure.

Rather than seeing it as a negative outcome, try to view it as an opportunity to learn and grow. Failure is a natural part of the learning process, and by embracing it, you can develop resilience and perseverance.

REMAINING CALM THROUGH CONFLICT

Designation: Emotional Intelligence, Conflict Resolution

LESSON:

Maintain a calm demeanour in conflict situations. If you have to yell or shout to get your point across, it is already lost, and your message may be lost in the noise. In any conflict, it's essential to remain composed and maintain a calm demeanour. When emotions run high, it can be tempting to raise your voice to assert your point. However, this approach often leads to further escalation of the conflict and makes it more difficult to reach a resolution. Instead of succumbing to anger and frustration, take a step back and try to approach the situation objectively. Speak clearly and calmly, and listen actively to the perspectives of others. By demonstrating emotional intelligence and self-control, you can help to de-escalate the conflict and find a mutually beneficial solution. Remember, it's always more effective to lead by example and communicate in a way that is respectful and constructive.

ACTION STEPS:
- *Listen actively:* When in conflict with someone, it's important to listen actively and try to understand their perspective. This can help you see the situation from their point of view

and find common ground, reducing the intensity of the conflict. By listening actively, you can also show the other person that you respect their opinions and are willing to work toward a resolution.

- *Take a break:* If the conflict is becoming too intense, taking a break and stepping away from the situation for a while can be helpful. This can give you time to calm down and gather your thoughts, as well as provide a chance for both parties to cool off and revisit the conflict with a clearer head. By taking a break, you can avoid getting too caught up in the emotion of the moment and revisit the conflict in a more rational and constructive way.
- *Practise mindfulness:* One of the best ways to remain calm in the face of conflict is to practise mindfulness. This involves focusing on the present moment and staying aware of your thoughts and emotions without getting caught up in them. By staying grounded and present, you can avoid getting overwhelmed by the intensity of the conflict.

YOU ARE WHAT YOU MAKE YOURSELF OUT TO BE

Designation: Identity, Self-Reflection

LESSON:

You are what you make yourself out to be, and people will treat you as you teach them to treat you. You are the creator of your own identity and the master of your fate. The person you become, the life you lead, and how others treat you is largely determined by the choices you make and the actions you take. You have the power to shape who you are and how others perceive you, and it's up to you to take responsibility for your own life and make the necessary changes to achieve your goals and live the life you want. The way you present yourself and the boundaries you set for others can have a significant impact on the way others treat you. If you project confidence, assertiveness, and a strong sense of self, others are more likely to treat you with respect and take you seriously. On the other hand, if you are passive, indecisive, and lack self-esteem, others may take advantage of you and treat you poorly.

For this reason, it is essential to set clear boundaries and communicate effectively with others. Speak up when someone is crossing your boundaries and communicate clearly and concisely. This will help establish a strong sense of self and assertiveness, and others will be more likely to treat you with the respect and consideration you deserve. You should also respect the boundaries of others and treat them with kindness and empathy. Take control of your life, and remember you have the power to create the life you want and live it on your own terms.

ACTION STEPS:
- *Set clear boundaries:* To avoid being mistreated, it's important to set clear boundaries for yourself and communicate them to others. This might include saying no to requests that don't align with your values or priorities, speaking up when someone crosses a line or violates your trust, or establishing clear expectations for how you want to be treated in a particular relationship or situation.
- *Practise assertive communication:* Assertive communication is a key tool for taking control of how people treat you. This involves expressing your thoughts, feelings, and needs in a clear, direct, and respectful way while also listening to and

considering the perspectives of others. By practising assertive communication, you can establish yourself as someone confident, self-assured, and deserving of respect.

- **Be selective about who you surround yourself with:** Finally, it's important to be selective about who you allow into your life. Surrounding yourself with positive, supportive, and respectful people can help reinforce your self-worth and encourage others to treat you with the same care and consideration. When you encounter people who consistently mistreat you or disregard your boundaries, it may be necessary to distance yourself from them or end the relationship altogether.

IMPORTANCE OF REPUTATION

Designation: Personal Branding, Image

LESSON:

Building a good reputation or image takes a lot of time, effort, and consistent behaviour. People pay close attention to how you act and make decisions, and are quick to form opinions about you based on these observations. When you consistently act with integrity, good sense, and professionalism, you'll find that people start to view you in a positive light. They'll trust you more, respect you more, and feel confident they can rely on you.

However, it only takes one moment of poor judgment or a single act of irresponsibility to damage the positive image you have worked hard to build. People quickly forget the good things you have done when they perceive you to have failed. If you make a mistake or act in a way that goes against your principles, it can leave a lasting impact on others' opinions of you. That is why it is crucial to always act with good sense and integrity, no matter the situation. Be mindful of your words and actions and ensure they align with your values and principles. This means being responsible for your mistakes and taking steps to make amends. Treat others with respect and dignity, even when you disagree with them or things get difficult. By always acting with good sense and integrity, you will build a reputation you can be proud of and that will serve you well in all areas of life.

ACTION STEPS:

- *Be mindful of how you present yourself:* Take care to present yourself in a positive manner, whether it's in person or online. Make an effort to be polite, honest, and reliable in your interactions with others.
- *Build and maintain positive relationships:* This can help establish a strong support network and increase opportunities for personal and professional growth.
- *Take responsibility for your actions:* If you make a mistake or experience a setback, take responsibility and work to make things right. This can help prevent long-term damage to your reputation and demonstrate your commitment to doing the right thing.

DEFINITION OF SUCCESS

Designation: Self-Awareness, Self-Reflection

LESSON:

Success is a subjective concept and varies from person to person. When you share your plans and aspirations with others, it's not uncommon to encounter differing opinions on what constitutes success. This can be frustrating, especially if the other person's definition of success doesn't align with your own.

It's important to surround yourself with people who share a similar mindset and understanding of success. In a community of like-minded individuals, you can foster a healthy competition of success and growth. The pressure to succeed is high, but it's the kind of pressure that motivates and inspires you to reach new heights.

Being in a supportive environment of people with similar aspirations allows you to push each other forward, encouraging each other to pursue your individual goals while growing collectively. The competition between you and your colleagues or friends becomes a positive force that helps everyone rise. In this environment, it's possible to find success in ways you never thought possible. The key is to align yourself with those who have similar goals, as they can provide guidance, support, and accountability when you need it most. By working together and pushing each other to achieve success, you can unlock new levels of growth and fulfilment that you may have never thought possible.

ACTION STEPS:

- *Define your own mindset:* Before you can find people with similar mindsets, it's important to define your own. Take

some time to reflect on your values, beliefs, and goals. Write them down and use them as a guide to help you identify others who share your mindset.
- *Join communities:* Look for communities or groups that align with your mindset. This could be a professional organization, a hobby group, or an online community. Engage with others in these communities and actively seek opportunities to connect with those who share your values and goals.
- *Attend events and meetups:* Attend meetups and events such as a seminar, a conference, or a workshop that focuses on topics related to your mindset. These events allow you to network and meet others who share your interests and values. Be open to connecting with others and follow up with those with whom you feel a connection.

EMBRACE UNCERTAINTY AND THE UNKNOWN

Designation: Personal Development, Growth

LESSON:

Embracing uncertainty and the unknown is critical to personal growth and development. Life is unpredictable, and no matter how much we try to control it, there will always be variables beyond our control. The key is learning to be comfortable with the unknown and embracing the uncertainty that comes with it. This means being open to new experiences, taking risks, and being willing to face the unknown without fear or hesitation. One of the benefits of embracing uncertainty is that it allows us to develop resilience and adaptability. When faced with uncertainty, we have to learn to think on our feet, make quick decisions, and adapt to changing circumstances. This ability to adapt is critical in our personal and professional lives, and it can help us navigate even the most challenging situations with grace and confidence.

Embracing uncertainty also allows us to approach life with curiosity and wonder. When we are open to new experiences and willing to explore the unknown, we open ourselves up to new ideas, perspectives, and ways of thinking. This can lead to personal growth, creativity, and innovation as we are exposed to new information and challenged to think outside the box. Of course, embracing uncertainty is not always easy. It can be uncomfortable and scary to step into the unknown, requiring us to let go of our need for control and predictability. However, when we learn to embrace the uncertainty that comes with life, we open ourselves up to new possibilities and opportunities for growth and self-discovery.

ACTION STEPS:
- *Practise mindfulness:* Mindfulness involves being present in the moment without judgment. By practising mindfulness, you can learn to become more aware of your thoughts and feelings and learn to accept them without judgment. This can help you become more comfortable with uncertainty and the unknown.
- *Take calculated risks:* While uncertainty can be uncomfortable, taking calculated risks can help you grow and learn. Start by taking small risks, such as trying a new hobby or reaching out to someone new. As you become more comfortable with uncertainty, you can take bigger risks that may lead to greater rewards.
- *Cultivate curiosity:* Cultivating curiosity can help you approach the unknown with an open mind. Ask questions,

try new things, and seek out new experiences. You can learn and grow in ways you never imagined by approaching the unknown with curiosity.

ALIGNING ACTIONS WITH PERSONAL VALUES AND BELIEFS

Designation: Personal Growth, Self-Awareness

LESSON:

As human beings, we have the capacity to think about and reflect on our values and beliefs—something essential to do if we want to live a meaningful and fulfilling life. Values and beliefs are the foundation of our identity and shape our perception of the world around us. They are the guiding principles that determine our thoughts, actions, and decisions. It is important to take time to reflect on our values and beliefs because they can change over time. We may adopt new values and beliefs or discard old ones, depending on our experiences and the people we interact with. By regularly considering and evaluating them, we can ensure that they align with our current understanding of the world and our goals in life.

Once we have identified our values and beliefs, aligning our actions with them is essential. This means making choices and decisions consistent with our values and beliefs. If we act in a way that is inconsistent with our values, we may experience internal conflict and cognitive dissonance, leading to dissatisfaction and unhappiness. Aligning our actions with our values and beliefs requires conscious effort and self-awareness. It requires us to regularly assess our actions and decisions and make adjustments when necessary. It also means being willing to stand up for our values and beliefs, even when difficult or unpopular.

ACTION STEPS:
- *Reflect on your values and beliefs:* Consider what is most important to you in life, what you stand for, and what motivates you. This can help you to gain a better understanding of yourself and what drives you.
- *Identify areas of misalignment:* Once you have reflected on your values and beliefs, identify areas where your actions may not align with them. Consider any discrepancies between your actions, values, and beliefs, and be honest with yourself about where you may be falling short.
- *Develop a plan:* Develop a plan to align your actions with your values and beliefs. Identify specific steps you can take to bring your behaviour into closer alignment with your beliefs. This may involve making changes to your daily routine, setting new goals, or seeking new opportunities more in line with your values.
- *Be patient and persistent:* Remember that aligning your actions with your values and beliefs is a process that may take time to see progress. Be patient with yourself, and stay committed to your goals even when it feels challenging. With persistence and dedication, you can achieve a greater sense of alignment between your values and actions, leading to a more fulfilling and purposeful life.

INDEPENDENCE AS AN ASSET

Designation: Self-Reliance, Individuality

LESSON:

Gaining independence in life in both personal and career capacities is a crucial step toward becoming a greater asset, whether you're working alone or as part of a team. Independence allows us to take control of our lives and make meaningful progress toward our goals. In a personal capacity, independence means being able to take care of ourselves, our families, our households, and our mental state. This might involve developing financial literacy, learning how to cook, managing household finances, or navigating other aspects of daily life. By gaining independence in these areas, we can lead a more self-sufficient life and reduce our reliance on others. In a career capacity, independence means being able to take charge of our professional lives and make progress toward our goals. This might involve developing new skills, seeking new opportunities, or taking the initiative to launch our own businesses. By becoming more self-sufficient and capable in our careers, we can make a greater impact and contribute more to the success of our companies, organizations, and society as a whole.

Independence also allows us to be more sustainable in our personal and professional lives. When we are self-sufficient and capable, we are less likely to rely on others for support and can make progress toward our goals without relying on external factors. Working as part of a team also becomes easier when we have independence in our personal and career lives. By having a solid foundation and a clear understanding of our capabilities, we can work effectively with others and contribute to the success of the team. Our independence allows us to bring unique perspectives and skills to the table, making us valuable assets.

ACTION STEPS:

- *Take ownership of your life:* To gain independence, it's important to take ownership of your life. This means accepting responsibility for your actions, decisions, and outcomes. Take the time to reflect on your goals, values, and priorities, and make decisions that align with these. Remember that you are in control of your life, and taking ownership is the first step to gaining independence.
- *Build your skills and knowledge:* Developing a wide range of skills and knowledge can help you gain independence and become an asset in life. Take the time to learn new things, whether it's through formal education, online courses, or self-directed learning. Seek opportunities to practise and apply your skills, and look for ways to build a portfolio of achievements and accomplishments.
- *Build a support network:* Finally, building a support network of like-minded individuals can help you gain independence and become an asset. Look for mentors or coaches who have experience in your area of interest, and engage with a community of like-minded individuals who can offer feedback and support. A support network can provide you with guidance, encouragement, and new perspectives, all of which can help you achieve your goals and gain independence.

PRIDE IN YOUR ACTIONS

Designation: Pride, Personal Fulfilment, Self-Esteem

LESSON:

When you look at your life, it's important to consider the bigger picture. The actions you take and the choices you make aren't just affecting you in the present moment; they also have the potential to ripple out and shape the future for generations to come. With this in mind, it's crucial to make choices you can be proud of. Think about the long line of your family history and the people who came before you. They may have faced different challenges and obstacles, but they all had one thing in common: they wanted to make the world a better place for their children and future generations. You have that same opportunity and responsibility. When you act with integrity and purpose, you are continuing your family's legacy and building a brighter future for those who come after you.

But it's not just about your family. Your actions also impact the people around you and the world as a whole. You have the power to make a positive difference, which is something to be proud of. Whether through your work, relationships, or community involvement, strive to make a meaningful impact and take pride in your actions. By doing so, you can live a life you can look back on with satisfaction and fulfilment, knowing that you made a difference in the world. It's important to reflect on the choices and decisions you make, and how they align with your values and beliefs. When considering the legacy you want to leave behind, it's essential to think about the impact your actions will have on future generations. The people who came before you have contributed to who you are today, and it's your turn to carry that legacy forward in a positive way.

If you can say with certainty that your actions are ones you can be proud of and that future generations can look back on them with admiration and respect, then you are on the right path. Maintaining high standards for yourself takes effort and dedication, but the reward is a sense of purpose and fulfilment. The choices you make every day, from the way you treat others to the work you do, all contribute to your overall character. By taking pride in your actions, you demonstrate to yourself and those around you that you hold yourself to a high standard and are willing to put in the work necessary to live up to it.

ACTION STEPS:

- *Set goals:* Setting specific, measurable goals can help you take actions that align with your values and aspirations. Identify the values and areas of your life that you want to improve, and set goals that align with these areas. You can feel a sense of pride and accomplishment when you achieve these goals. (Very repetitive, I know. I simply cannot stress the importance of setting goals and setting more once you've completed the previous ones. You might see this one in other lessons to come.)
- *Celebrate your successes:* Take time to acknowledge and celebrate your successes, no matter how small. Celebrating your successes can boost your confidence and sense of self-worth and help you feel proud of your actions. Celebrations don't have to be big—they can be as simple as treating yourself to a small reward, like a favourite snack or a relaxing activity.
- *Practise self-reflection:* Regularly reflecting on your actions can help you learn from your mistakes and identify areas for improvement. Set aside time to reflect on your day or week, and ask yourself questions like, "What did I do well today?"

and "What could I have done better?" Use these insights to make changes to your behaviour and take actions that align with your values.

SEEING THE GOOD IN ALL SITUATIONS

Designation: Positivity, Optimism

LESSON:

It's easy to focus on the negative aspects of a situation and overlook the positive, but seeing the good in all situations is a crucial aspect of personal growth and development. When faced with adversity or challenges, it's essential to adopt a positive and proactive mindset and look for opportunities for growth and learning within the situation.

By seeing the good in all situations, you can cultivate a more optimistic outlook on life. You can look beyond the immediate difficulties and focus on the long-term benefits of the experience. This mindset shift can help individuals approach challenges and obstacles with a more positive and proactive attitude, leading to greater success and fulfilment in the long run. Furthermore, seeing the good in all situations can improve relationships and foster greater empathy and understanding. When you adopt a positive and constructive perspective, you are more likely to engage with others in a more meaningful and productive way. You will be able to see the best in others and communicate in a way that encourages cooperation and collaboration.

Adopting a mindset of seeing the good in all situations can be a valuable asset in life. It requires a strong sense of discipline, mental toughness, and the ability to maintain a positive outlook in the face of adversity. By focusing on the positive aspects of a situation, you can improve your own well-being and have a more meaningful impact on those around you.

Don't wait for good things to come your way—actively seek opportunities to improve your circumstances and grow as a person. Look for ways to turn challenges into opportunities, and don't be afraid to take risks and embrace new experiences. Focus on what you are grateful for and cultivate a mindset of abundance and optimism. Surround yourself with positive, supportive individuals and develop strong, meaningful relationships. By maintaining a sense of perspective, seeking new opportunities, and adopting a positive attitude, you can cultivate a mindset of positivity and resilience that will serve you well throughout your life.

ACTION STEPS:

- *Practise gratitude:* See the good in all situations. Take time each day to reflect on what you are grateful for, no matter how small. Focusing on the positive can help shift your perspective and help you find something good in even the most challenging situations.
- *Reframe your thoughts:* Look for the silver lining in every situation. Instead of dwelling on the negative aspects of a situation, try to find the positive. Ask yourself, "What can I learn from this experience?" or "How can I use this situation to grow and improve?"
- *Practise self-compassion:* Be kind and compassionate to yourself when facing difficult situations. Treat yourself with the same kindness and understanding you would offer a friend. This can help you develop resilience and always remain encouraged.

APPRECIATE THE JOURNEY, NOT JUST THE DESTINATION

Designation: Mindfulness

LESSON:

Appreciating the journey, not just the destination, is an important concept to remember when pursuing goals or objectives. It's easy to get caught up in the result, but we often forget that getting there is just as important. The journey is where you learn, grow, and develop as an individual. It's where you face challenges and obstacles that force you to adapt, learn new skills, and push yourself to improve. By focusing solely on the destination, you run the risk of missing out on the valuable lessons the journey has to offer. It's important to take time to reflect on the progress you have made and appreciate the small victories along the way. When you learn to appreciate the journey, you are better equipped to handle setbacks and obstacles you will encounter along the way.

Appreciating the journey can also help you to stay motivated and focused on your goals. When you can see the progress you have made and appreciate the hard work you have put in, it can give you a sense of purpose and drive to continue moving forward. It also helps to cultivate a positive mindset and outlook on life, as you learn to embrace the process and find joy in the journey rather than just the end result. It's about finding value and meaning in the process. It helps you stay motivated, learn and grow, and develop a positive mindset that can help you overcome obstacles and setbacks.

ACTION STEPS:

- *Practise mindfulness:* Mindfulness involves paying attention to the present moment without judgment. By practising mindfulness, you can become more aware of your thoughts and feelings and learn to appreciate the present moment. You can practise mindfulness through meditation, breathing exercises, or simply by paying attention to your surroundings.
- *Set process-oriented goals:* Instead of focusing solely on the end result, try setting goals that focus on the process. For example, if you're learning a new skill, set a goal to practise for a certain amount of time each day rather than focusing on mastering the skill right away. By setting process-oriented goals, you can enjoy the journey of learning and growing rather than just focusing on the end result.
- *Embrace uncertainty:* Life is full of uncertainty, and learning to embrace it can help you appreciate the journey. Instead of fearing the unknown, approach it with curiosity and openness. Embracing uncertainty can help you stay flexible and open to new opportunities and experiences.

LIVE WITH INTENTION AND PURPOSE

Designation: Personal Development, Social Responsibility

LESSON:

Living with intention and purpose is the foundation of a meaningful and fulfilling life. It means taking responsibility for your existence and striving to positively impact the world around you. To live with intention and purpose, you must first identify your values and goals and then align your actions with them. This requires self-reflection, introspection, and a willingness to be honest with yourself. Once you have identified your values and goals, you can begin to take deliberate actions that will move you closer to achieving them. This may involve making sacrifices, taking risks, and stepping outside your comfort zone. It may also require a willingness to learn, grow, and adapt as circumstances change.

Living with intention and purpose is not always easy. You will encounter challenges, setbacks, and obstacles along the way. However, by staying focused on your goals and values and continuing to take deliberate and intentional actions, you can overcome these challenges and create a truly meaningful and fulfilling life.

ACTION STEPS:

- *Identify your values:* Your values are the principles and beliefs that guide your life. By identifying your values, you can clarify what is most important to you and use this knowledge to guide your decisions and actions. Take some time to reflect on your values and write them down. Then, make a conscious effort to live in alignment with them.
- *Set meaningful goals:* Setting goals that are meaningful and aligned with your values can help you stay focused and motivated.
- *Take action:* This is the key to living with intention and purpose. Once you have identified your values and set meaningful goals, take action to bring them to life. This might mean volunteering in your community, taking on a leadership role at work or in your personal life, or simply being kind and compassionate toward others. Whatever actions you take, make sure they are aligned with your values and goals.

Learn to lift others. Do not fear that they will grow to outshine you. Embrace it. If you stay on your own path then they, and you, will grow together.

PROBLEM-SOLVING

"Between stimulus and response there is a space. In that space is our power to choose our response. In our response lies our growth and our freedom."

—VIKTOR FRANKL

WELCOME TO A NEW CHAPTER ON PROBLEM-SOLVING—A critical skill essential for success in any area of life. In this chapter, we will explore the principles, strategies, and practical steps to help you develop a problem-solving mindset, overcome challenges, and achieve results. Life is filled with challenges, obstacles, and complexities that often leave us feeling overwhelmed or stuck. However, the power of effective problem-solving lies in its ability to transform these challenges into opportunities for growth, innovation, and success. Whether you're facing a personal or professional challenge, problem-solving is a crucial skill that can empower you to take control of the situation and find solutions that move you forward.

Problem-solving is not just about finding quick fixes or temporary solutions. It's about developing a mindset that embraces challenges as opportunities to learn, adapt, and grow. It requires critical thinking, creativity, and the ability to approach problems with a solution-oriented mindset. This chapter will delve into the mindset, principles, and strategies that will equip you with the tools to become an effective problem solver in any situation.

As you navigate through the following lessons, you will learn actionable steps, practical tips, and real-life examples that will help you apply problem-solving techniques to your unique circumstances. From identifying root causes and generating creative solutions to implementing and evaluating their effectiveness, each lesson will provide valuable insights to sharpen your problem-solving skills and achieve tangible results. Problem-solving may sometimes require stepping out of your comfort zone, confronting difficult situations, and making tough decisions. It may demand resilience, perseverance, and a willingness to learn from failures. However, the rewards of effective problem-solving are immeasurable. It's about finding innovative solutions, achieving breakthroughs, and creating positive change in your life and the lives of others.

I urge you to approach this chapter on problem-solving with a proactive mindset, a willingness to learn, and a commitment to taking action. Remember, this is not just a skill but a mindset you can develop and refine over time. So, get ready to embrace challenges, develop effective problem-solving skills, and achieve meaningful results. The journey continues.

THERE ARE RESOURCES FOR EVERY TASK

Designation: Problem-Solving, Resourcefulness

LESSON:

Remember that the resources are available for nearly every imaginable task or goal you want to undertake. In today's world, access to information and resources has never been easier. Whether you're looking to learn a new skill, start a new project, or reach a personal goal, a wealth of information is available. With the power of the internet, books, articles, and other resources at your fingertips, you can find information on nearly any topic you can imagine.

The wealth of information available to us is empowering and amazing to comprehend. Suppose you're interested in learning a new language, for example. In that case, you can find countless resources online that can help you achieve your goal—from language-learning apps to online courses and video tutorials, there's no shortage of resources available. If you can't find the answer you're looking for, you can find forums, discussion groups, or even live tutors who can help you find a solution.

The same is true for just about any task or goal. Whether you're looking to start a new business, learn how to cook, or write a book, everything you need is available.

ACTION STEPS:

- *Do your research:* One of the first steps in understanding that resources are available for every task is to do your research. Take the time to explore the task or problem you are facing and investigate the available resources. This could include online articles, books, videos, podcasts, and more.

- ***Seek out experts:*** Experts in the field can be a valuable resource when completing a task or solving a problem. Look for experts and seek out their advice or guidance. This could include attending workshops or seminars, joining a professional organization, or contacting individuals in the field for advice.
- ***Collaborate with others:*** Collaborating with others can help you discover new resources and approach a task from multiple angles. Seek individuals with experience or expertise in your area of interest and engage in collaborative projects or discussions. By working with others, you can pool your resources and knowledge to find effective solutions.

QUESTION EVERYTHING—BUT IN THE RIGHT WAY

Designation: Problem-Solving, Critical Thinking

LESSON:

Question everything—but in the right way, so you do not come off as annoying but also learn everything you possibly can. Asking questions is an essential part of learning and personal growth, but it's important to do so in a way that is respectful and considerate of others. When it comes to questioning things, it's all about striking a balance. On the one hand, you want to ask enough questions to thoroughly understand a situation or issue. On the other hand, you don't want to appear overly aggressive, pushy, or annoying. The key is to approach questions in a curious and genuine manner, rather than aggressive or critical.

One effective way to approach questioning is to adopt a continuous learning mindset. Whether you're in a new job, starting a project, or engaging with a new group of people, try to maintain an open and curious mindset. Ask questions with the goal of gaining a better understanding, and be respectful and considerate of others as you do so. Another approach is to frame questions to show your interest and investment in the situation. For example, instead of simply asking, "Why did this happen?" try asking, "Can you help me understand more about what led to this outcome?" This type of question shows that you're not just looking to place blame or find fault but also to gain a deeper understanding of the situation.

Ultimately, it's important to remember that questioning everything is not about being skeptical or distrustful but rather about being proactive and engaged in the process of learning and discovery. If approached correctly, asking questions can lead to a deeper understanding of the world around us and help us make better decisions and improve our personal and professional lives.

ACTION STEPS:

- *Ask open-ended questions:* When questioning something, ask open-ended questions inviting discussion and exploration. This can help you better understand the issue and encourage others to share their perspectives and insights.
- *Seek out diverse perspectives:* To question everything in the right way, it's important to seek diverse perspectives and opinions. This can help you gain a more well-rounded understanding of the issue and avoid falling into a narrow mindset. Engage with people who have different experiences, viewpoints, and backgrounds to gain a deeper understanding of the issue.
- *Use critical thinking:* Critical thinking is the process of

evaluating information and arguments to make informed decisions. When questioning things, it is important to use critical thinking to evaluate the validity and reliability of the information you're presented with. This can help you make informed decisions based on reliable evidence and avoid falling for misinformation.

THE IMPORTANCE OF ASKING QUESTIONS

Designation: Learning, Curiosity

LESSON:

On the same note as the previous lesson, asking questions is a crucial aspect of engaging with others and gaining insight into their perspectives and experiences. It opens the door to meaningful conversations and the opportunity to expand one's understanding of the world and the people in it. Asking questions also demonstrates your interest in the person and their life, which can be a significant source of validation for others. However, it is essential to approach this practise with sensitivity and respect. Not everyone may be comfortable discussing personal topics, and it's important to respect their boundaries and not push them into sharing more than they are willing to. Additionally, it is essential to be aware of cultural and social norms and understand what topics may be inappropriate in certain settings.

It's important to balance asking questions and actively listening to the responses. It's not just about gathering information, but also about building relationships and connecting with others on a deeper level. When you ask questions and listen with genuine interest, you show that you value the person and what they have to say, and that can foster trust and respect in your interactions.

Additionally, asking questions is a form of self-education. The more you ask, the more you learn and expand your knowledge and understanding of the world and the people around you. By actively engaging with others and asking questions, you can challenge your beliefs and perspectives and grow as an individual. Asking questions is also a valuable skill to have in both personal and professional relationships. It opens the door to new experiences and opportunities and helps to build strong, meaningful connections with others. Moreover, when you listen with a genuine interest and an open mind, people are more likely to trust and respect you, leading to more fulfilling relationships in all aspects of life.

ACTION STEPS:

- *Be curious:* The first step in asking effective questions is to be genuinely curious. Approach each conversation or situation with an open mind and a desire to learn more. This means actively listening to others, asking follow-up questions, and being receptive to new information and ideas.
- *Be specific:* When asking questions, it's important to be as specific as possible. This means asking questions that are tailored to the situation and that seek to elicit specific information or insights. For example, instead of asking a general question like, "How's the project going?" you might ask a more specific question like, "What's the status of the marketing campaign?"
- *Ask open-ended questions:* Finally, it's important to ask open-ended questions that encourage discussion and exploration. This means asking questions that can't be answered with a

simple yes or no, but require more thoughtful and nuanced responses. Open-ended questions might begin with phrases like, "What do you think about..." or "Can you tell me more about..." By asking open-ended questions, you'll be able to engage in more meaningful conversations and gain a deeper understanding of the topic.

MULTIPLE WAYS TO DO THINGS

Designation: Problem-Solving, Creativity

LESSON:

There are multiple ways to do things. Only on rare occasions is there only one single "right" way. This is because success is subjective, and what works for one person may not work for another. On the same note, just because one person is right doesn't mean another is wrong. It's always important to consider where someone is coming from in their approach to a task or idea since everyone comes from different backgrounds and brings experiences that can alter how they go about something. Be sure to be open to allowing those around you to try or explain why they do something differently—it may just be better than your approach.

The notion that there is only one "right" way to do things can also stifle creativity and innovation. When people fall into this way of thinking, they become afraid to think outside the box and try new things. Considering this will allow you to embrace the idea that there are multiple ways to solve problems. Explore new possibilities and opportunities.

ACTION STEPS:

- *Explore different perspectives:* To better understand multiple ways to take on challenges, it's important to explore different perspectives. Seek out people who have faced similar challenges and learn from their experiences. Take the time to listen to their stories, ask questions, and consider how their approach to the challenge might differ from your own.
- *Embrace creativity:* Being creative in problem-solving can help you see challenges in new and different ways. Rather than relying on the same tried-and-true solutions, take the time to brainstorm new and innovative ways to approach the challenge. Try techniques such as mind mapping or freewriting to generate new ideas and explore different possibilities.
- *Build a network of individuals:* Finally, build a network of people who can offer guidance and support when faced with a challenge. Seek mentors or coaches with experience in your area of interest, and engage with a community of like-minded individuals who can offer feedback and support. A support network can provide you with multiple perspectives and help you see a challenge from different angles.

NOTING THOUGHTS FOR FUTURE IMPROVEMENT

Designation: Self-Improvement Habits

LESSON:

Writing your thoughts is a powerful tool for organizing and clarifying your ideas. Whether you're crafting a business proposal, writing a book, or composing an email, getting your thoughts down on paper can help you find the words and structure you need to communicate effectively. When faced with a blank sheet of paper, it can be overwhelming to know where to begin. But sometimes, the best approach is to simply start writing. Don't worry about getting everything right at first; simply put your thoughts down on paper and let the ideas flow.

Once you've written down your thoughts, you can then take the time to clean up your words and reorganize your ideas into a coherent sequence. This process allows you to clarify your thoughts, refine your arguments, and find the best way to present your ideas. Whether you're writing for work, personal growth, or any other reason, writing your thoughts and cleaning up your words is a critical step toward effective communication. By giving yourself the space to think and create, you'll be able to articulate your ideas clearly and concisely, ensuring your message is heard loud and clear.

ACTION STEPS:

- *Freewrite:* Freewriting is a technique where you write continuously for a set period without worrying about grammar, spelling, or punctuation. The goal is to generate ideas and write your thoughts down without judgment. Freewriting can help you clarify your ideas by allowing you to explore different angles and perspectives without self-censorship.
- *Mind mapping:* This visual technique organizes your thoughts and ideas. Start by writing down your central idea or topic, then create branches of the central idea with related subtopics. From there, add more branches with specific details, examples, and supporting evidence. Mind mapping can help you see the connections between ideas and identify gaps in your thinking.
- *Revising:* Revision is the process of rethinking and refin-

ing your ideas. After you have written your first draft, take the time to revise it with fresh eyes. Read through your work and look for areas where your ideas may be unclear or underdeveloped. Consider different perspectives and challenge your assumptions. Revising can help you clarify and make your ideas more focused and coherent.
- *Phone notes:* Additionally, you can make a note on your phone for anything that sparks an interest. If you title a note with a subject of interest for a project, hobby, or other related matter, then that alone will have you constantly thinking of the related subject.

THE "WE'VE ALWAYS DONE IT THIS WAY" MINDSET

Designation: Problem-Solving, Willingness for Change

LESSON:

Don't get stuck in the "But we've always done it this way" mindset in a workplace or any other area of life. If something has been done a certain way for some time, it means it was—and still could be—effective, but also that it may be time to reassess and see if it's still the most productive way of doing things or if it could be improved upon. Continually look for more effective ways to do things, even if they require more time or effort. This shift in mindset highlights the importance of being open-minded and flexible in one's approach to life and work. This stuck-in-the-box thinking can be especially prevalent in a workplace setting, where established routines and procedures often take on a life of their own.

Remember that just because something has been done a certain way does not necessarily mean it is the best or most effective way of doing things. By embracing a curious mindset, you will often find that many long-standing practises are outdated and ineffective and that there are more efficient and effective ways to achieve goals. Both critical thinking and a willingness to embrace change can be the key to unlocking greater success and satisfaction in your personal and professional lives.

ACTION STEPS:
- *Challenge assumptions:* To overcome a stubborn mindset, it's important to challenge assumptions. Ask yourself why things are done a certain way and if there might be a better or more efficient way to achieve the same result. Don't be afraid to question established practises and seek out new approaches.
- *Embrace change:* Change can be difficult, but staying current and competitive is often necessary. Rather than clinging to old practises, be open to change and innovation. Look for opportunities to improve processes, streamline workflows, and be willing to take risks and try new approaches.
- *Encourage feedback and input:* It's important to encourage feedback and input from others. Seek out diverse perspectives and be open to new ideas and approaches. Foster a culture of continuous improvement where employees are encouraged to question established practises and suggest new ways of doing things. This can help you stay agile and responsive to changing circumstances and avoid becoming stagnant or outdated.

DO NOT GET CARRIED AWAY BY EMOTIONS

Designation: Attention to Detail, Future Problem-Solving

LESSON:

One of the most common mistakes we make about important life decisions is getting carried away by our emotions and overlooking potentially important details. This can happen in various situations, whether it's a new relationship or a career opportunity that seems too good to be true. The problem with acting impulsively based solely on emotions is that it can blind us to the facts and lead us to decisions that may not be in our best interest in the long run. To make sound decisions that will set us up for a successful future, we need to detach from our emotions and take a sober and objective look at the situation.

This means examining the present, past, and future states of the situation. In the present state, you need to look at the facts and details immediately available. What are the key features of the relationship or career opportunity, and what do they entail? What are the potential benefits and drawbacks of pursuing this path? In the past state, you need to look at the history of the situation. What were the experiences of other people who pursued similar relationships or careers? What were the successes and failures in the past? Are there any red flags or warning signs you need to be aware of?

Finally, in the future state, you need to think about the potential long-term consequences of your decisions. Where might this path lead you in five, ten, or twenty years? What are the potential risks and rewards of pursuing this path? Will this decision lead you closer to your goals, or will it take you off track? By taking a sober and objective approach to assessing your options, you can make better decisions in alignment with your values and goals. This requires you to put aside your emotions and biases and focus on the facts and details essential to making a sound decision. It may not be easy, but it is vital if you want to create a fulfilling and successful life.

ACTION STEPS:

- *Take your time:* It's important to avoid rushing into things too quickly. Resist the urge to make hasty decisions based on initial impressions or excitement. Instead, take the time to carefully consider your options, weigh the pros and cons, and make an informed decision.
- *Do your research:* Whether you're considering a new career opportunity or a new relationship, it's important to do your research. Take the time to learn more about the company or person you're considering. Look for red flags, read reviews or ask for references, and gather as much information as possible before deciding.
- *Ask questions:* Don't be afraid to ask questions, especially regarding important details. Whether you're in an interview or on a date, ask thoughtful questions that can help you better understand the person or opportunity you're considering. This can help you make a more informed decision and avoid overlooking potentially important details.
- *Seek advice:* Consider seeking advice from someone you trust, such as a mentor, friend, or family member. They may be able to offer a different perspective or provide insights you hadn't considered. This can be especially helpful if you feel unsure or overwhelmed by the decision-making process.

STEPPING BACK FROM SITUATIONS TO ASSESS PROPERLY

Designation: Self-Awareness, Mindfulness

LESSON:

Similar to the previous lesson, it is natural to become invested in a problem or project, often leading to unnecessary emotions and confusion. It is important to recognize when it is necessary to take a step back and reassess the situation objectively. By doing so, you can gain a fresh perspective, avoid tunnel vision, and see the logic and possible solutions or next steps. Stepping back also helps to detach emotions, which can cloud your judgment and prevent you from finding effective solutions. This can help you approach a task or conflict with a clearer mind, leading to better outcomes.

When you find yourself becoming overwhelmed, take a break, take a walk, meditate, or simply do something to clear your mind. When you return to the task, you will be refreshed and better equipped to tackle it. This is a valuable strategy to develop, as it helps to reduce stress and maintain mental clarity. Moreover, it is always helpful to have someone you trust provide an outside perspective and offer guidance. Sometimes, discussing the situation with a neutral third party can help you see things in a new light and find creative solutions.

Taking a step back and reassessing a situation is a key strategy for solving problems and making progress in any task or conflict. By doing so, you can prevent emotions and confusion from clouding your judgment and see things objectively, leading to better outcomes.

ACTION STEPS:

- ***Take a break:*** When you feel overwhelmed or emotionally charged, take a break. It could be a few minutes or a few days, depending on the situation. Use this time to clear your head and gain some perspective. This will allow you to come back to the situation with a fresh outlook and a clearer mind.
- ***Practise mindfulness:*** Mindfulness is a practise that helps you stay present in the moment and observe your thoughts and emotions without judgment. Practising mindfulness teaches you to step back from situations and assess them more objectively. Start by practising mindfulness meditation for a few minutes each day, and gradually increase the duration as you become more comfortable.
- ***Seek input from others:*** When you're unsure how to assess a situation, seek input from others. Talk to people you trust who have a different perspective, and who can offer advice and support. This will help you see the situation from different angles and make a more informed decision.

LIFE AS A COMPLEX MAZE

Designation: Problem-Solving, Strategic Thinking

LESSON:

Life can often be considered a complex maze, full of twists and turns that make it difficult to navigate. When faced with a difficult problem or a goal, it can be tempting to approach it head-on, trying to forge ahead and find the solution. This approach can often lead to confusion, frustration, and feeling lost and not knowing how to move forward.

Just as working through a maze from the end to the beginning on paper can be more straightforward, sometimes working backward from an issue can be a more effective strategy. By starting with identifying the problem or goal you have in mind and working backward, you can understand the steps you need to take to get there. This approach also allows you to identify the underlying causes of the problem, which can help you find more permanent solutions. It can also reveal alternative paths that you may have previously overlooked and allow you to consider multiple solutions before committing to a particular course of action.

Working backward from an issue can be a powerful tool for problem-solving and can help you gain clarity and focus on your endeavours. By embracing this approach, you can simplify complex problems and find effective solutions, even when the path ahead may appear confusing or uncertain. It's important to approach each challenge with a flexible mindset and be open to new ways of thinking and approaching problems. When working backward, it's essential to be thorough and consider all possible starting points, no matter how small or insignificant they appear. It's also important to remain focused and patient as you work backward, avoiding the urge to jump ahead to potential solutions before thoroughly exploring all possible starting points. Take the time to examine the situation from multiple perspectives and gather all the information you need to make informed decisions.

By approaching challenges in this way, you can develop a more comprehensive understanding of the problem at hand and be better equipped to find practical solutions. Additionally, by working backward, you can learn to think creatively and challenge conventional wisdom, which can help you find innovative solutions to even the most complex problems. By embracing this approach, you can gain a deeper understanding of the world around you and be better equipped to navigate the maze of life with confidence and purpose.

ACTION STEPS:
- *Identify the problem:* The first step in working backward from issues is to identify the problem. Clearly define the issue and its impact on your life or work. This can help you better understand the root cause of the problem and identify potential solutions.
- *Determine the root cause:* Once you have identified the problem, determine the root cause. Ask yourself why the problem is occurring and what factors are contributing to it. This can help you identify the underlying issues causing the problem and allow you to address them directly.
- *Develop a plan:* Finally, develop a plan to address the problem. Start by defining what success looks like and what steps you need to take to achieve it. Break the plan down into smaller, manageable tasks and assign responsibilities. Set specific timelines for each task and track progress regularly. Remember to remain flexible, as unexpected challenges may arise, but stay focused on the end goal and adjust the plan to ensure success. By working backward from the issue, you can identify the root cause and develop a targeted plan to address the problem and achieve your goals.

If it's done with, don't dwell on it, learn from it.

COMMUNICATION AND INTERPERSONAL SKILLS

"Always do what is right. It will gratify half of mankind and astound the other."

—MARK TWAIN

WELCOME TO THE NEXT CHAPTER ON COMMUNICATION AND Interpersonal Skills—two fundamental aspects of human interaction that can make or break our personal and professional relationships. In this chapter, we will explore the principles, strategies, and practical steps to help you become a more effective communicator and develop strong interpersonal skills.

Effective communication and interpersonal skills are essential for success in today's world. Whether you're dealing with colleagues, clients, friends, or family, communicating clearly, listening actively, and connecting with others is critical for building healthy relationships and achieving your goals. However, communication breakdowns, misunderstandings, and conflicts can cause unnecessary pain and strain in our relationships, hindering our ability to achieve our desired outcomes.

The good news is that communication and interpersonal skills can be learned, developed, and improved. It's not just about the words we say but how we say them, how we listen, and how we connect with others on a deeper level. In this chapter, we will explore the mindset, principles, and strategies to help you enhance your communication and interpersonal skills to resolve conflicts, build trust, and achieve positive outcomes in your interactions with others. Throughout this chapter, you will gain actionable insights, practical techniques, and real-life examples that will empower you to apply effective communication and interpersonal skills in various situations. From active listening and empathy to assertiveness and conflict resolution, each lesson will provide valuable tools to navigate the complexities of human interaction and build meaningful connections with others. Mastering communication and interpersonal skills may require stepping out of your comfort zone, being vulnerable, and developing new habits. It may demand self-awareness, emotional intelligence, and a willingness to constantly learn and improve. However, the rewards of effective communication and strong interpersonal skills are immeasurable. These abilities are about fostering meaningful relationships, building trust, and achieving mutual understanding and cooperation with others.

I encourage you to approach this chapter with an open mind, a willingness to practise, and a commitment to taking action. Remember, communication and interpersonal skills are not just tools but a way of being that can transform your relationships and elevate your interactions with others. So, prepare to enhance your communication skills, develop strong interpersonal skills, and achieve positive outcomes in your personal and professional interactions.

The journey continues.

THE USE OF WORDS AS TOOLS

Designation: Communication, Influence

LESSON:

Words are incredibly powerful tools. They can transport you to places you have never been, evoke emotions you have never felt, and bring about change in the world. When used with precision and purpose, the right words can profoundly impact those who hear them. They can inspire, motivate, and bring people together, or they can divide, hurt, and cause harm. The key to harnessing the power of words lies in understanding the way they are used and the context in which they are spoken. Words can shape the way we see the world, and they can shape the way others see us. They can bring us closer to our goals and aspirations, or they can hold us back and keep us from reaching our full potential. A well-crafted sentence, delivered with conviction, can move mountains. The tone, energy, and intention behind our words are critical components of their effectiveness.

Therefore, choosing our words carefully, using them wisely, and speaking with purpose is crucial. The right combination of words, spoken with the right energy, tone, and intention, can have a lasting impact on the world. They can create a legacy that will live on long after we are gone. So, let us embrace the power of words, use them with care, and create a better world for us all.

ACTION STEPS:

- *Practise effective communication:* The foundation of using words as tools to achieve everything in life is effective communication. This involves developing the skills to express yourself clearly and persuasively and listening actively and attentively. Take time to practise your communication skills, and seek feedback and advice from others to help you improve.
- *Be intentional with your language:* The words you choose can have a powerful impact on your ability to achieve your goals. Be intentional with your language, and choose positive, empowering, and motivating words. Avoid negative self-talk and language that undermines your confidence or self-esteem.
- *Develop a growth mindset:* Finally, it's important to develop a growth mindset when using words as tools to achieve everything in life. This involves embracing challenges as opportunities for growth and viewing failures as learning experiences rather than setbacks. Adopt a growth mindset and use language that encourages and motivates you to persevere and continue striving toward your goals, even in the face of adversity.

BEING HONEST WITH YOUR INTENTIONS

Designation: Self-Awareness, Interpersonal Communication

LESSON:

Being truthful and transparent in your intentions is an essential aspect of building trust and credibility with others. When you are honest about what you want and what your goals are, people are more likely to believe in you and trust you. This, in turn, can lead to stronger relationships, both personally and professionally, as well as improved collaboration and teamwork. Furthermore, being honest about your intentions can save you time and energy that would otherwise be spent on fabrication and manipulation. When truthful, you don't have to worry about maintaining a façade or keeping track of lies. This lets you focus on more important things, such as your work and relationships.

Honesty and transparency can also help to create a positive work environment. When people are open and honest with each other, they can avoid misunderstandings and resolve conflicts more quickly. This, in turn, can improve overall productivity and lead to better outcomes. Honesty is necessary to build trust, credibility, and positive relationships with others. Being truthful and transparent can save you time and energy, improve your relationships, and help you lead a more fulfilling life.

ACTION STEPS:

- *Take time to reflect on your intentions:* Before communicating your intentions to others, take the time to reflect on what you truly want to achieve. This can involve identifying your underlying motivations, values, and priorities. By gaining clarity on your intentions, you can communicate them more effectively and with greater authenticity.
- *Communicate your intentions clearly:* When communicating your intentions to others, be clear and direct. Use simple, straightforward language that is easy for others to understand. Avoid being vague or ambiguous, as this can create confusion or distrust. When communicating your intentions, make sure to also listen to the other perspective and be open to feedback.
- *Align your actions with your intentions:* This means follow-

ing through on your commitments and being consistent in your behaviour. When your actions align with your intentions, you demonstrate your integrity and build a reputation for being trustworthy. If your intentions change, communicate them openly and honestly to those affected, and adjust your actions accordingly.

BEING A BETTER LISTENER

Designation: Interpersonal Communication, Personal Development

LESSON:

When people complain or vent their problems to you, there's a good chance they just want someone who can listen. If they ask for a solution or your thoughts on the matter, you can have something prepared through active listening, but that won't always be the case. In most instances, after someone vents a concern, they are generally happy with comments agreeing with their frustration. Too often, we begin to utter multiple possible fixes to someone's problem, only to find out that was not what they really wanted. The art of active listening is crucial in developing meaningful relationships, both professionally and personally. You show others they are valued and heard by truly hearing and understanding what they are saying. This can increase trust and strengthen bonds, leading to more productive and fulfilling interactions.

It is important to remember that effective communication is a two-way street. While it may be tempting to jump in and offer solutions or advice, it's important first to understand the root of the issue and what the other person is truly seeking. You can achieve understanding through active listening, imagining the situation from their perspective, and asking questions. Whether in the workplace or our personal lives, the benefits of effective communication and active listening cannot be overstated.

To be a great listener means being present in the moment and paying close attention to the words and emotions of the person speaking. It requires setting aside our own thoughts and concerns and making a genuine effort to understand and connect with the other person. This type of active listening leads to deeper and more meaningful conversations and can help to build stronger relationships. Moreover, practising active listening can have a profound impact on our own well-being and happiness. When we make a conscious effort to truly listen and understand others, we open ourselves up to new perspectives and experiences. We can gain valuable insights and wisdom from those around us. It can also help us to develop empathy and compassion and connect with others on a deeper level. By practising active listening, we can build stronger relationships, gain valuable insights and wisdom, and enrich our lives in the process.

> **Note:** We are all guilty of wasting effort in meaningless conversations or in important conversations, simply preparing our next words in our minds as the person in front of us speaks, causing us not to hear or embrace the importance of their words. People you encounter will feel more essential in your presence in the moment if you appear to fully acknowledge what they are saying. In an engaging conversation, it is acceptable to pause after actively listening to respond appropriately. Whether you are empathetic or feigning empathy, it would benefit you to imagine a situation happening to you to relate to an individual. There are two types of empathy that are worth considering:
>
> **Cognitive empathy**, which is an understanding of how others think and feel.
>
> **Emotional empathy**, which involves feeling the emotions of others.

ACTION STEPS:

- *Practise active listening:* Active listening means focusing on the speaker and truly hearing what they say. To practise active listening, give the speaker your full attention, make eye contact, and avoid interrupting or talking over them. Summarize what the speaker said in your own words to ensure you understand them correctly.
- *Practise empathy:* Empathy is the ability to understand and share the feelings of others. To become a better listener, practise putting yourself in the speaker's shoes and imagining how they feel. This can help you connect with the speaker more deeply and understand their perspective more fully.
- *Avoid distractions:* Distractions can interfere with your ability to listen effectively. Turn off your phone and other electronic devices, find a quiet space to listen, and avoid multitasking while someone is speaking. By removing distractions, you can focus on the speaker and be fully present in the conversation.
- *Ask open-ended questions:* Asking open-ended questions can help you better understand the speaker's perspective and engage in more meaningful conversation. Ask questions that invite the speaker to share more about their thoughts and feelings, such as, "How did that experience make you feel?" or "What do you think about that?"
- *Practise nonjudgment:* Avoid judging the speaker or their ideas, and approach the conversation with an open mind. Listen without preconceptions or biases, and be willing to consider the speaker's perspective even if you disagree. Practising nonjudgment can create a safe and open space for meaningful communication.

ASKING QUESTIONS OFTEN AND EARLY

Designation: Communication, Interpersonal Skills

LESSON:

When starting a new position in or outside a work environment, ask as many questions as possible. It can be frustrating when an employer or trainer says you should be asking questions but you don't know what you don't know. However, consider this: given the information you already know, imagine scenarios that can occur and ask the outcome or resolution if you do not know what that would be. This can help you to identify areas where you may need more information or training. Try to ask the more minor questions early on, as asking them later could make you appear unknowledgeable. Remember that if you do not know something within the timeframe you should know it, then there is no better time than the present to learn. Admitting that you don't know everything can be humbling, but it also shows that you're humble and willing to learn. By asking questions, you can better understand your role and the expectations for your performance. Remember, there might be a look of confusion or judgment, but it's always better to ask a question than make a mistake.

Starting a new position can be overwhelming, especially when there's so much to learn and many questions to ask. It's important to remember that everyone has to start somewhere, and asking questions is a crucial part of the learning process. By asking questions, you can gain a deeper understanding of your responsibilities and the expectations for your role. It's natural to feel frustrated when you're told to ask questions, but when it comes down to it, you don't know what you don't know. To overcome this, think about scenarios that may arise in your role and ask about the outcome or resolution to those scenarios if you're unsure. This can help you to identify areas where you may need more information or training.

Asking questions can also help build trust and establish positive relationships with coworkers and superiors. They will appreciate your initiative and genuine interest in doing your job well. It also demonstrates your commitment to your role and willingness to go the extra mile to ensure you're fully equipped to perform to the best of your abilities. Questions can also lead to opportunities for growth and development. By seeking information and knowledge, you're expanding your skillset and opening yourself up to new experiences and challenges. This can help to enhance your personal and professional growth and set you on a path to success.

ACTION STEPS:

- *Prepare questions in advance:* Before attending a meeting or starting a new project, consider what information you need to know. Write down a list of questions you can ask to clarify any uncertainties. This will help you feel more prepared and confident when you ask questions.
- *Listen actively:* When someone is speaking, make sure to listen actively and take notes. This will help you remember the key points and formulate better questions. Additionally, actively listening to what others are saying can help you avoid asking questions that have already been addressed.
- *Don't be afraid to ask for clarification:* If you don't understand something, don't be afraid to ask for clarification. It's better to ask for clarification early on than wait until it's too late to make changes. When you ask for clarification, be specific about what you don't understand and why you need

more information. This will help the other person provide a more tailored response.

THE WAY YOU WORD THINGS

Designation: Communication, Interpersonal skills

LESSON:

Work on how you word things. The cadence, tone, and words you use can drastically affect the conversation's outcome. Effective communication is key to achieving your goals. Words have immense power, and it is essential to choose them wisely. When engaging with people, it is crucial to reflect positivity in your words and tone. This will help build rapport and make the person you're speaking with more inclined to assist you in your goals. If you approach someone aggressively or confrontationally, they will be less likely to want to help you. On the other hand, if you present your case calmly and professionally, they are more likely to listen and understand where you're coming from.

In critique or discipline, the way you word things is equally important. It's natural to want to soften the blow when delivering difficult news, but it's important to be straightforward and clear in your communication. If you sugarcoat the issue, it can lead to confusion and hinder the chances of your recipient understanding the point you're trying to convey. Instead, approach the situation with empathy and aim to find a solution that works for both parties. By paying attention to the tone, cadence, and words used, you can positively impact the outcome of any conversation, build rapport with people, and easily achieve your goals.

ACTION STEPS:

- ***Be clear and concise:*** When communicating with others, try to be as clear and concise as possible. Use simple language and avoid jargon or technical terms others may not understand. Consider using examples or analogies to help illustrate your point.
- ***Consider your audience:*** When choosing your words, consider who you are speaking to and their background or knowledge. Tailor your language to fit their level of understanding and try to anticipate any questions or concerns they may have.
- ***Practise active listening:*** Effective communication is a two-way street. Make sure to actively listen to what others are saying and respond in a way that acknowledges their concerns or perspectives. This can help build rapport and trust and make it easier to communicate effectively in the future.

BEING STRAIGHTFORWARD

Designation: Communication, Interpersonal Skills

LESSON:

Be straightforward with people. It'll save you time and effort from trying to gloss over details to make them feel better. People will appreciate you more for knowing you care enough to be honest with them, although they may not immediately acknowledge it. Honesty and directness are key principles that should guide your life. Being straightforward with people demonstrates your commitment to their well-being and respect for their time and emotions. It can be tempting to sugarcoat the truth or avoid difficult conversations, but in the long run, it is much more efficient and effective to just be honest. Being honest also helps build trust and strengthen relationships. Honesty is not just about telling the truth but also about being clear and concise in your communication. By avoiding ambiguity, you reduce the chance of misinterpretation and confusion.

In a professional setting, being straightforward can also be a competitive advantage. Your colleagues and superiors will appreciate your clarity, and your clients will value your honesty. Being straightforward also shows that you are confident in your abilities and believe in your work. Whether you are dealing with a difficult customer, negotiating a deal, or working on a challenging project, straightforwardness is a quality that will set you apart and help you succeed.

Ultimately, this trait is a sign of maturity and respect. It shows that you are responsible, trustworthy, and that you take your relationships and responsibilities seriously. So, be proud of your straightforwardness and embrace it as a defining characteristic of who you are and what you stand for.

ACTION STEPS:

- *Identify your goals and intentions:* Before entering any conversation or situation, take a moment to clarify your goals and intentions. This will help you communicate your message clearly and directly.
- *Speak clearly and directly:* When communicating, use clear and concise language to get your point across. Avoid using overly complex language or sugarcoating your message, as this can lead to misunderstandings and confusion.
- *Practise active listening:* Being straightforward is not just about speaking your mind; it's also about listening actively to others. When someone is speaking to you, focus on what

they are saying and give them your full attention. This will help you respond more thoughtfully and directly to their needs and concerns.

UNDERSTANDING EMOTIONS IN INTERACTIONS

Designation: Emotional Intelligence, Interpersonal Skills

LESSON:

When it comes to our interactions with others, it's important to understand the motivations behind our emotions and feelings. Why do we feel the way we do about a particular person or situation? Is it because we have high expectations for them or because we're envious of their success? It's important to take a step back and analyze these feelings to communicate effectively with others. If you're feeling frustrated with someone, try to explain why you feel that way, if possible. This will help the other person understand where you're coming from and make them more likely to change their behaviour or attitude for the better. Remember, the goal is to build better relationships, not to tear others down.

It's essential to understand why you feel the way you do and how those feelings may impact others. If you have frustration toward a colleague, it's important to handle the situation with empathy and respect. Approach the situation with a desire to understand their perspective and communicate your own clearly and constructively. By doing so, you can work toward finding a solution and strengthening your relationship with them.

Furthermore, it's crucial to recognize that everyone has their own strengths, weaknesses, and growth areas. If you hold someone to a high standard, it's important to understand that this may not be their current reality. Encourage and support them, help them see their potential, and provide resources for their growth. It takes time and effort to grow and change, and a positive and supportive environment can make all the difference. When approaching situations with empathy and respect and working toward finding solutions, you can create a positive and supportive environment for growth and improvement.

ACTION STEPS:

- *Practise active listening:* Active listening involves not only hearing the words someone is saying but also paying attention to their facial expressions, body language, tone of voice, and emotions. Make a conscious effort to focus on the person speaking, and ask clarifying questions to ensure you understand what they're saying. By actively listening, you can better understand their perspective and emotions.
- *Develop emotional intelligence:* Emotional intelligence refers to the ability to understand and manage one's own emotions and those of others. To develop your emotional intelligence, you can practise self-awareness by reflecting on your own emotions and how they impact your interactions with others.
- *Communicate effectively:* Effective communication involves expressing your emotions and needs while also acknowledging and respecting those of others. When interacting with others, be clear and direct in your communication, and try to express your emotions constructively. Also, make an effort to be aware of others' emotions and respond in a way that shows empathy and respect. By communicating effectively, you can build stronger relationships and avoid misunderstandings and conflicts.

PERSPECTIVES OF OTHERS IN DISAGREEMENTS

Designation: Interpersonal Skills, Emotional Intelligence, Effective Communication

LESSON:

Disagreements are an inevitable part of any social interaction, including in the workplace. It is important to approach these situations with an open mind and to consider the perspectives of others. There may be times someone else has a better plan or approach to a task, and you should be willing to listen and consider their ideas. It is also important to be mindful of situations where someone's mission may be to derail you or get ahead at your expense. This can happen in competitive environments, where individuals or teams are vying for limited resources or opportunities. In these cases, it is essential to maintain a vigilant and critical stance and to be aware of the motives and intentions of those around you.

   To effectively navigate these situations, strong communication skills are important, as well as the ability to articulate your own ideas and perspectives clearly and persuasively. You must also have a deep understanding of your values and priorities and be able to defend them when necessary. Ultimately, it is about finding a balance between considering the perspectives of others and maintaining your own position and goals. By doing so, you can maintain a strong sense of purpose and direction and avoid being swayed or misled by those with different agendas.

ACTION STEPS:

- *Practise empathy:* Empathy is the ability to understand and share the feelings of others. To consider the perspectives of others, it's important to practise empathy. Try to put yourself in their shoes and see the situation from their point of view. This can help you better understand their perspective and build stronger relationships.
- *Ask open-ended questions:* When trying to consider the perspectives of others, it's important to ask open-ended questions. These questions encourage people to share their thoughts and feelings rather than just giving a yes or no answer. This can help you gain a deeper understanding of their perspective and build trust.
- *Be open-minded:* To truly consider the perspectives of others, it's important to be open-minded. This means being willing to listen to different viewpoints and being open to changing your own perspective based on what you learn. Avoid making assumptions or jumping to conclusions. Instead, take the time to really understand where others are coming from.

ABILITY TO VIEW FROM MULTIPLE PERSPECTIVES

Designation: Flexibility, Open-Mindedness

LESSON:

The ability to view things from multiple perspectives and take different approaches is a crucial aspect of effective problem-solving and decision-making. Our first instincts can be correct in many cases, but it's also essential to be open to new ideas and alternatives. When faced with a challenge or decision, it's important to consider multiple perspectives and take a variety of approaches. This means looking at the problem from different angles, seeking out new information, and being open to alternative solutions.

Incorporating the opinions and ideas of others is also essential in this process. Collaboration and teamwork can lead to better outcomes and can provide new insights and perspectives you may not have considered. Incorporating the opinions and ideas of others can also bring new perspectives and insights that can lead to better outcomes. However, it's important to maintain the discipline to make the final decision and not simply rely on the opinions of others.

It's important to approach this process with a critical outlook. Not every idea or suggestion is valid, and it's essential to carefully weigh the pros and cons of each approach before making a final decision. When faced with a challenge, you should have the discipline to step back, assess the situation, and consider all options before making a final decision. This requires listening to others, gathering information, and seeking new ideas and alternatives. The ability to view things from different angles and take different approaches is a critical aspect of leadership and success. You'll be better equipped to navigate complex situations and achieve your goals by approaching challenges and decisions with a disciplined and informed mindset.

ACTION STEPS:
- *Practise empathy:* This can help you understand their motivations, concerns, and experiences and see how these might be different from your own. To practise empathy, try actively listening to others and asking open-ended questions to understand their perspectives.

- *Challenge your assumptions:* We all have assumptions and biases that can colour our perceptions and prevent us from seeing situations from different perspectives. Ask yourself what evidence supports your assumptions and what evidence contradicts them. Seek out diverse perspectives and viewpoints to broaden your understanding of a situation.
- *Use critical thinking:* Using critical thinking can help you see situations from different perspectives by examining the evidence from multiple angles. To use critical thinking, try breaking down a situation into its parts and considering each part in isolation. Use evidence and reasoning to evaluate each part, and then draw a conclusion based on the totality of the evidence. By using critical thinking, you can develop a more nuanced and objective understanding of a situation.

ADMITTING WHEN YOU DON'T KNOW SOMETHING

Designation: Effective Communication, Self-Awareness

LESSON:

Admitting when you don't know something is an essential aspect of personal growth and maturity. It shows humility and the willingness to learn, two traits that are highly valued in any individual. Furthermore, having an open mind and admitting when you don't know something can help you avoid getting trapped in a bubble of your own beliefs and opinions, which can limit your intellectual and personal growth.

On the contrary, having heavily weighted opinions on things you don't know much about can be damaging, not only to yourself but also to those around you. It can lead to misunderstandings, conflicts, and a lack of progress in finding solutions to problems. For example, if someone has a strongly held opinion on a topic about which they have little knowledge, they may not be open to alternative perspectives and ideas. This can lead to a closed-minded approach and rejection of potentially valuable insights.

Having a heavily weighted opinion on things you don't know much about can also harm your reputation and credibility. People are less likely to trust and respect individuals who present themselves as experts on subjects they have little to no knowledge of. Furthermore, spreading incorrect information or having opinions that are not based on facts can be harmful to those who rely on you for guidance or information. It is important to acknowledge when you don't know something and to avoid having heavily weighted opinions on things you don't know much about. Admitting that you don't know something opens the door to new opportunities for learning and growth while avoiding the pitfalls of having ill-informed opinions. Instead, strive to be knowledgeable and informed on the topics that matter to you, and always be willing to admit when you don't know something.

ACTION STEPS:

- *Acknowledge your knowledge gaps:* Recognize that admitting you don't know something is not a sign of weakness or incompetence but rather a strength. Acknowledge your knowledge gaps, and understand there is always more to learn. By doing so, you open yourself up to new ideas and possibilities and create opportunities for growth and development.
- *Ask for help:* When you don't know something, don't be

afraid to ask for help. Seek guidance from mentors, colleagues, or subject matter experts. Be specific about what you don't know and need help with. This can help you to quickly fill knowledge gaps and move forward with greater confidence.

- *Take ownership of your learning:* Take ownership of your learning and development by actively seeking new information and skills. To expand your knowledge and skills, engage in ongoing professional development opportunities, such as training sessions or online courses. Stay curious and open to new ideas, and seek feedback from others to continue improving. By taking ownership of your learning, you can build your confidence, increase your knowledge, and ultimately become a more effective and valuable team member.

BEING HONEST, EVEN IF IT HURTS YOU

Designation: Integrity, Effective Communication

LESSON:

Honesty is a cornerstone of integrity and is essential to building trust with others. But sometimes, being honest can have consequences, and it may not always be easy. The temptation to sugarcoat the truth or avoid difficult conversations may be strong, but it's important to be honest, even if it does damage in the short term. When you're honest with others, you establish a level of trust that is difficult to break. People appreciate honesty, even if they don't always like what they hear. And when you're honest, you're also being true to yourself, which is essential for personal growth and self-improvement. However, being honest can also have short-term consequences. For example, being honest about a mistake you made at work may result in disciplinary action or even the loss of your job. If you're honest about your feelings in a relationship, it may lead to an argument or even a breakup.

In the long run, being honest is always the best policy. When you're honest, even if it does damage in the short term, you create a foundation of trust that will pay off in the long run. You may have to face difficult consequences, but you can move forward with a clear conscience, knowing you did the right thing. It isn't always easy, and it takes courage to be truthful, even when difficult. But honesty is essential to building strong relationships, both personally and professionally. When you're honest, even if it hurts, you demonstrate your character and commitment to doing the right thing, no matter what. Don't be afraid to face the consequences of your honesty, and always strive to be true to yourself and others.

ACTION STEPS:

- *Acknowledge the situation:* When faced with a situation where honesty is difficult, it's important to acknowledge the situation and your feelings. Recognize that honesty may be uncomfortable or even painful, but that it's necessary for your own integrity and for the well-being of others. Take a deep breath, stay calm, and remind yourself of the importance of being honest.
- *Be direct and clear:* Avoid sugarcoating or beating around the bush, which can often lead to confusion and mistrust. Instead, be clear about your intentions and your message. Be mindful of your tone and language, and strive to communicate your message respectfully and compassionately.
- *Take responsibility:* When being honest hurts you, taking

responsibility for your actions and words is important. Be willing to accept the consequences of your honesty and take steps to address any negative outcomes. This may involve apologizing, making amends, or working to repair damaged relationships. By taking responsibility for your actions, you can build trust and respect with others, even in difficult situations.

DO NOT PUNISH FOR HONESTY

Designation: Trust, Transparency, Effective Communication

LESSON:

Honesty is a crucial component of any healthy relationship or situation. When someone is brave enough to come forward and admit their mistakes or experiences, it shows a level of integrity you should respect and appreciate. By punishing people for honesty, you risk sending the message that speaking the truth is not valued and will result in negative consequences. This can lead to a lack of trust and an environment where people cannot speak openly. However, it is important to remember that honesty does not always mean immunity from consequences. Depending on the circumstances, discipline may still be necessary. The key is to handle these situations with empathy and understanding. Let the person know that you appreciate their honesty, and take the time to consider the situation before deciding on the appropriate course of action.

When you show people that honesty is valued, they will be more likely to come to you in the future with any concerns or issues. They will know that they can trust you to listen and respond in a way that considers the bigger picture. By fostering a culture of honesty and openness, you can create a more productive and positive environment for everyone involved. Those who are punished with understanding, even if disciplined, will respect and appreciate you all the more. People willing to admit their mistakes and take responsibility are the ones you want around, and it's important to encourage and support them.

ACTION STEPS:

- *Encourage honesty:* To create an environment where honesty is valued and respected, it's important to encourage it. Let people know that you appreciate and respect their honesty, even if it means hearing something difficult. Thank them for sharing their thoughts and feelings with you, and acknowledge the courage it takes to be honest.
- *Listen without judgment:* When someone is honest with you, it's important to listen without judgment. Avoid becoming defensive or dismissive, even if you disagree with what was said. Allow the person to express themselves fully and ask questions to clarify their perspective. This can help you better understand their point of view and create a foundation of trust and mutual respect.
- *Address behaviour, not honesty:* If someone is honest with you about something that is not in line with your expectations or values, it's important to address the behaviour, not the honesty. Avoid punishing or blaming the person for being honest, and instead focus on finding a solution to the problem. This can help create a safe and supportive environment where honesty is valued and mistakes can be learned from and corrected. Remember, honesty is the foundation of trust, and healthy relationships are difficult to maintain without trust.

GIVING CREDIT WHERE CREDIT IS DUE

Designation: Interpersonal Communication

LESSON:

Giving credit where credit is due is an important aspect of leadership and teamwork. Giving others credit is about acknowledging and recognizing the contributions of others and being grateful for their efforts. When people feel valued and appreciated, they are more likely to be motivated and engaged and more likely to put in the effort necessary to achieve their goals. Leaders who give credit where credit is due inspire their team members to perform at their best. By recognizing the achievements of others, they create a positive work environment that fosters growth and encourages collaboration. When everyone feels valued, they are more likely to work together and support each other, resulting in a more productive and cohesive team.

In addition, giving credit where credit is due builds trust and respect among team members. When you acknowledge others' contributions and show gratitude for their work, you demonstrate that you trust them and believe in their abilities. This helps to establish a positive working relationship and builds a foundation for effective collaboration. Acknowledging people is important to building strong relationships, fostering collaboration, and achieving success. It shows respect for others, builds trust, and inspires others to perform at their best. Always make sure to give credit where it is due and recognize the contributions of others.

ACTION STEPS:

- *Acknowledge contributions publicly:* When someone has contributed to your success or achieved something noteworthy, acknowledge their contributions publicly. This can be a simple thank-you or a public recognition ceremony, depending on the situation. By publicly acknowledging someone's contributions, you not only make them feel appreciated but also inspire others to do their best work.
- *Use inclusive language:* When talking about group achievements, use inclusive language that acknowledges the contributions of all team members. Avoid using "I" statements exclusively and instead focus on using "we" statements to highlight the collective effort that led to success. Be specific in your acknowledgements, highlighting the specific contributions of different team members where possible.
- *Follow up with private recognition:* In addition to public acknowledgements, make sure to follow up with private recognition as well. This can be in the form of a personal thank-you note or a small token of appreciation. By recognizing contributions privately, you can strengthen relationships and build trust, leading to greater collaboration and productivity in the future.

ARTICULATING REASONS AND ACTIONS

Designation: Communication, Understanding

LESSON:

It is important to note that articulating the reasoning behind one's actions is beneficial for those around us and ourselves.

By explaining the reasoning and purpose behind what we do, we can ensure that our actions align with our values and beliefs. Furthermore, it allows us to reflect on our own thought processes and decision-making, helping us to become more self-aware and mindful. This ability to articulate our actions helps build trust and credibility in the eyes of others. When we can clearly explain our actions and decision-making, it demonstrates that we have put thought and consideration into our actions and we are confident in what we are doing.

Leadership and effective communication go hand in hand. Leaders who can articulate their intentions and actions inspire confidence and respect from their subordinates and colleagues. People are more likely to follow those whom they trust and respect, and this trust is built through clear and concise communication. In short, articulating our actions is essential for building trust, credibility, and understanding. It allows us to reflect on our own decision-making and become more self-aware, and it inspires those around us to believe in the cause and work toward a common goal.

ACTION STEPS:
- *Clarify your thoughts:* Take time to clarify your thoughts and emotions about a particular situation or decision. Journaling or talking with someone you trust can help you to organize your thoughts and articulate them more clearly.
- *Develop your communication skills:* Practise communication skills and learning through various methods: take courses or workshops, read books or articles, and seek feedback from others to improve your ability to articulate your reasons and actions.
- *Use concrete examples:* When explaining your reasons and

actions, use concrete examples to illustrate your points. This can help others understand your perspective and see the rationale behind your decisions.
- *Choose wording wisely:* Choosing wording wisely is important for articulating actions. Do not adopt a "Do that because I said so" attitude. If you were told to do something you have a vested interest in, wouldn't you want to know the reason why? People learn better and perform better if they believe in a cause. How can one put their all into a task they do not understand because a superior expects them to comply without knowing the meaning?

BEING AWARE OF SOCIAL SURROUNDINGS

Designation: Self-Awareness, Social Awareness

LESSON:

Being aware of your social surroundings requires focus and attention to detail. This means paying attention to the subtle cues and signals people give off, such as facial expressions and body language. When speaking with others, it's important to monitor their facial expressions to gauge their reactions to what you're saying. For example, if someone looks confused or uncomfortable, it may be a sign that you need to clarify or change your approach. It's also important to be mindful of the nonverbal cues you're sending. Your body language, tone of voice, and facial expressions can all impact how others perceive you and the message you're trying to convey.

In addition to focusing on facial expressions, it's also important to pay attention to other aspects of your surroundings, such as the tone of conversations, body language, and overall mood of a group or crowd. By being aware of these subtle cues, you can better understand a situation's dynamics and respond appropriately and effectively. Being socially aware requires practise and effort, but with time and dedication, it can become second nature and greatly enhance your relationships with others.

ACTION STEPS:

- *Practise active listening:* One of the best ways to become more aware of your social surroundings is to practise active listening. When you're in a social setting, consciously try to fully engage with the people around you. This means giving them your full attention, listening to what they're saying, and being present. By doing this, you'll be more aware of the social dynamics and cues in the environment.
- *Observe nonverbal cues:* In addition to listening to what people are saying, pay attention to their nonverbal cues. Nonverbal communication, such as body language and facial expressions, can often provide valuable information about a person's emotional state and can give you clues about social context. By observing nonverbal cues, you'll be more aware of the unspoken dynamics in a social setting.
- *Reflect on your own behaviour:* Finally, it's important to reflect on your behaviour in social situations. Ask yourself questions like, "How do I come across to others?" and "Am I being respectful and attentive to the people around me?" By being mindful of your behaviour, you can become more aware of how you fit into the social context and how your actions may be influencing the behaviour of others. This can help you develop stronger social skills and become more adept at navigating various social situations.

REASONING WITH PEOPLE

Designation: Social Interactions, Communication

LESSON:

Some people can't be reasoned with, but most are reasonable at their core—this is an important truth about human nature. People have the potential to be reasonable, but a number of different factors can stifle this potential. At times, people may become entrenched in their beliefs and unable to see the logic behind another perspective. In these cases, the reason may seem to be lost. It is important to remember that the capacity for reason remains even in these cases. The challenge is finding a way to reach that core of reason, to tap into the part of the individual that is open to understanding and growth.

One approach is to appeal to a person's values and use empathy to connect with their experiences and emotions. By doing so, it becomes possible to find common ground and begin to build an understanding. Additionally, it can be helpful to address the underlying concerns and fears driving the person's behaviour as this can help to defuse conflict and promote cooperation. Another approach is to appeal to a person's sense of reason by using clear and concise arguments grounded in evidence. When presenting these arguments, it is important to use language that is accessible and easy to understand and avoid using technical terms or jargon that can confuse or frustrate the person you are trying to reach.

Ultimately, the goal is to reach a mutual understanding where both parties can engage in a productive and respectful dialogue. This requires a willingness to listen and to be open to the perspectives of others, even if those perspectives may differ from your own. By staying focused on this goal, it is possible to maintain a level of reason and civility in even the most challenging conversations.

ACTION STEPS:
- *Establish common ground:* The first step in reasoning with people is to establish common ground. Find areas of agreement and understanding, and use those as a starting point for your discussion. This can help build a foundation of trust and respect, making your message more likely to be heard.
- *Use evidence and logic:* This can help to make your argument more persuasive and compelling and increase the likelihood of persuading others with your message. Use data, statistics, and other evidence to support your position and logical reasoning to make your case.
- *Be respectful and empathetic:* Listen to the perspectives and opinions of others and seek to understand their point of view. Be mindful of your tone and language, and avoid being confrontational or dismissive. By demonstrating respect and empathy, you can build trust and credibility and increase the likelihood that others will be open to your message.

A PRINCIPLE OF EXCHANGES

Designation: Exchanges, Impact, Communication

LESSON:

> ### LOCARD'S PRINCIPLE
>
> "Wherever he steps, whatever he touches, whatever he leaves, even unconsciously, will serve as a silent witness against him. Not only his fingerprints or his footprints, but his hair, the fibres from his clothes, the glass he breaks, the tool marks he leaves, the paint he scratches... All of these and more, bear mute witness against him. This is evidence that does not forget. It is not confused by the excitement of the moment. It is not absent because human witnesses are. It is factual evidence. Physical evidence cannot be wrong, it cannot perjure itself, it cannot be wholly absent. Only its interpretation can err. Only human failure to find it, study, and understand it, can diminish its value."
>
> —PROFESSOR EDMOND LOCARD (1877)

Also known as the Locard Exchange Principle, this concept in forensic science states that every contact leaves a trace. In other words, whenever two objects or surfaces come into contact, they exchange materials, leaving behind physical evidence. This principle was first proposed by Edmond Locard, a French criminologist and forensic scientist, and is considered one of the foundational principles of forensic science.

Just as every contact leaves a trace, according to Locard's Principle, every interaction we have with others can profoundly impact both ourselves and those we meet. We can think of each person we encounter as an opportunity to exchange ideas, perspectives, and lessons. We can gain new insights and grow as individuals when we approach each interaction with an open mind and a willingness to learn. At the same time, we should also be aware that we have something to offer others. By sharing our experiences, insights, and knowledge, we can provide others with valuable lessons they can use to better themselves. Whether we're engaging in conversation with a friend, colleague, or stranger, we should always strive to be a source of inspiration and guidance for those around us.

In this sense, every interaction can be considered a two-way exchange of knowledge and lessons, with each person taking something away and leaving something behind. By embracing this principle, we can enrich our own lives and the lives of those we meet, creating a cycle of mutual growth and improvement. It's important to approach each interaction with an open mind and a humble attitude, recognizing that there is always something to learn and something to teach. When we approach others with curiosity and a willingness to listen, we create a space for meaningful exchange and growth.

It's also important to be mindful of the lessons we choose to take from others. While everyone can offer valuable insights, it's important to carefully consider the source and evaluate whether a particular lesson aligns with our values and goals. Similarly, when offering lessons to others, it's crucial to do so in a respectful and considerate way. Avoid imposing your ideas on others; instead, strive to share your experiences and knowledge in a way that empowers and inspires. By embracing this two-way exchange of lessons, we can foster meaningful connections with others, enhance our personal growth, and positively impact the world. It's a powerful principle that can help us to create a better, more connected, and more compassionate world, one interaction at a time.

ACTION STEPS:
- *Be mindful of your interactions:* Pay attention to how you interact with others, and be intentional about the messages you are sending, both verbally and nonverbally.
- *Cultivate empathy:* To fully appreciate the importance of every interaction, it's essential to cultivate empathy. This involves putting yourself in the other person's shoes and considering their perspective and needs. By doing so, you can develop a deeper understanding of the impact your interactions may have on others and adjust your behaviour accordingly.
- *Focus on creating value:* When interacting with others, focus on creating value. Whether intentional or not, every interaction involves giving and taking. By focusing on creating value for others, you can build a sense of trust and goodwill and create positive interactions that benefit everyone involved. This may involve offering assistance or support, providing useful information or insights, or simply showing appreciation and respect for the other person. By taking a value-focused approach to every interaction, you can help ensure your interactions are positive and productive and build meaningful connections with those around you.

> Never stop putting in the effort to reach your goal. The reward for success is worth it all.

VI.

PERSONAL RESPONSIBILITY

"A man's worth is no greater than the worth of his ambitions."
—MARCUS AURELIUS, *MEDITATIONS*

WELCOME TO THE NEXT CHAPTER ON PERSONAL RESPONSIbility—a foundational principle that can transform your mindset, empower you to take charge of your life, and create positive change. In this chapter, we will explore the concept of personal responsibility, its importance, and how it relates to your life and well-being.

Personal responsibility is about owning your actions, choices, and outcomes. It's about recognizing that you have the power to shape your life, regardless of circumstances or external factors. It's a mindset that acknowledges that you are in control of your destiny and that your choices have consequences. In today's fast-paced world, it's easy to blame others, external circumstances, or bad luck for our shortcomings or failures. Playing the victim, making excuses, or avoiding taking responsibility for our actions is tempting. However, this mindset only perpetuates a cycle of disempowerment, frustration, and unfulfilled potential. The truth is that personal responsibility is the antidote to victimhood. It's the foundation of success, resilience, and self-empowerment. When you embrace personal responsibility, you take ownership of your life, decisions, and results. You become the captain of your ship, charting your course and navigating through challenges with resilience and determination.

In this chapter, we will explore the principles and mindset of personal responsibility and how it can transform your life. We will delve into practical strategies, actionable steps, and real-life examples that will empower you to embrace personal responsibility and create positive life changes. It's important to note that personal responsibility is not about blaming yourself or others. It's not about perfection or avoiding mistakes. It's about taking ownership of your actions, learning from failures, and continuously improving. It's about cultivating a growth mindset, embracing challenges as opportunities for growth, and taking proactive steps toward your goals.

Throughout the lessons that follow, you will be challenged to reflect on your mindset, choices, and actions. You will be empowered to take responsibility for your life and make intentional decisions that align with your values and aspirations. You will be equipped with practical tools and strategies to overcome obstacles, develop resilience, and create a life of purpose and fulfilment. So, get ready to embrace personal responsibility, transform your mindset, and unlock your full potential. It's time to take charge of your life and create your desired future. Let's dive into the world of personal responsibility and discover its power for your personal growth and success.

SETTING ASIDE YOUR EGO TO LEARN

Designation: Personal Responsibility, Humility, Willingness to Learn

LESSON:

You should put your ego aside when actively learning from a superior, trainer, mentor, or other guiding presence. There is a balance, however, and you shouldn't give the impression that you do not know something you should know. Actively listen, acknowledge information, and do not hesitate to ask questions where needed. Set aside your preconceived notions and keep an open mind when learning new skills and tasks. It is important to be humble and at the mercy of your trainer or mentor. Even if you think you already know something, it will benefit you to keep your knowledge in mind and see if what you are being taught lines up with it, what could be applied for the better, and what could be applied differently.

Understand that learning is an ongoing process with room for growth and improvement. No one knows everything, and it's essential to admit that you may not know all the answers. Be open to new information. In this way, you create an environment of collaboration and growth for yourself and those around you.

Another aspect to consider is that being receptive to guidance and instruction from others demonstrates a level of respect and trust in their abilities and experience. It shows that you value their contributions and are willing to work together toward a common goal. This type of attitude can create a positive dynamic in any working relationship and foster a sense of teamwork and collaboration.

Moreover, it is crucial to approach learning with a growth

mindset and recognize that your abilities and understanding can be developed through dedicated effort and perseverance. Remember, acquiring knowledge and skills is a lifelong journey, and there is always room for improvement. The willingness to learn and grow is a key characteristic of successful individuals, and it will serve you well in all areas of life. Additionally, it is essential to be mindful of the source of information and knowledge you are receiving. Many individuals claim to be experts, but not all have the credentials or experience to back up their claims. Find credible sources, people with a proven track record who are well-respected in their field. Such individuals are invaluable resources and can provide valuable insights and advice to help you achieve your goals and aspirations. Furthermore, verify information and cross-reference with multiple sources to ensure the information you receive is accurate and trustworthy.

ACTION STEPS:

- *Acknowledge what you don't know:* The first step in setting your ego aside to learn is acknowledging what you don't know. This means recognizing that there's always more to learn and that you don't have all the answers. Embrace a growth mindset, and approach each new learning opportunity with a beginner's mind.
- *Listen actively:* When someone shares their knowledge or expertise, listen actively and attentively. This means paying close attention to what the other person is saying, asking follow-up questions, and seeking to understand their perspective. Avoid interrupting or talking over the other person, and resist the urge to dismiss their ideas or opinions.
- *Be willing to make mistakes:* Learning often involves making

mistakes, and it's important to be willing to make them. Don't be afraid to try something new or take a risk, even if it means you might fail. Embrace failure as an opportunity to learn and grow, and be open to feedback and constructive criticism. Remember that making mistakes is a natural part of the learning process and it's often through our failures when we discover our greatest successes.

REFRAIN FROM BLAMING OTHERS

Designation: Personal Responsibility, Accountability

LESSON:

When something occurs that is your fault or the fault of another, do not blame those under your command. If you are leading and a subordinate makes an error, ask yourself if you took the time to make sure they understood the task. If they have been given all necessary directions and still do not appear to comprehend the task, it may be time to find one that better suits them. It is important to remember that as a leader, your actions and decisions can create a ripple effect on those under your command. When mistakes are made, it is crucial to handle the situation in a manner that promotes accountability and growth. Blaming others for mistakes is not only ineffective, but it also undermines the trust and respect you have built with those you lead.

In instances where mistakes are made, it's important to first assess the situation and ask yourself if you did everything in your power to ensure that your subordinates understood the task. Did you provide clear instructions? Did you take the time to answer any questions they had? Did you adequately train and prepare them for the task? If you can answer yes to these questions, it may be time to reassess their capabilities and consider whether the task is a good fit for them. On the other hand, if you realize that you could have done more to ensure their understanding, then it is your responsibility to own up to it and work to prevent similar mistakes from happening in the future. This could mean providing additional training or resources or simply taking more time to communicate instructions.

In any case, it is crucial to approach situations with a growth mindset and focus on finding solutions rather than placing blame. This fosters a positive and productive work environment and helps to build a strong team.

ACTION STEPS:

- *Take responsibility:* Rather than pointing fingers at others, take ownership of your own mistakes and shortcomings. This can help shift the focus from assigning blame to finding solutions and moving forward.
- *Use "I" statements:* When discussing problems, use "I" and "we" statements instead of "you" statements. This can help prevent others from becoming defensive and instead foster a more collaborative approach to problem-solving.
- *Focus on solutions:* Rather than dwelling on past mistakes or assigning blame, focus on finding solutions to problems. This can help create a positive and productive environment and ensure everyone works toward a common goal.

VICTIM MINDSETS

Designation: Personal Responsibility, Self-Empowerment

LESSON:

The tendency to play the role of the victim can be tempting, especially when life throws us curveballs or presents us with challenges. However, it is important to understand that life will not always be easy, and everyone has their own struggles and battles to face. Instead of feeling sorry for ourselves and complaining about our problems, we should seize opportunities, work hard, and build positive relationships with those around us. To live a fulfilling life, we must actively work to shape our own destinies, making the most of what we have and taking advantage of the opportunities presented to us. While it is important to acknowledge and understand our experiences and struggles, it is equally important not to let them define us or limit our potential.

Victim mentality is often accompanied by a sense of entitlement, making it difficult to see the world in a positive light and find meaning in life. By recognizing that everyone has their own battles and focusing on our own growth and self-improvement, we can avoid falling into the trap of playing the victim. Instead, we can work toward building resilience and developing the skills necessary to overcome adversity and live a meaningful life. It is essential to understand that playing the victim not only detracts from one's agency and ability to shape their own life but it also undermines the struggles and hardships of others. When we focus on what has gone wrong in our lives or what we believe to be injustices, we fail to see the present opportunities. This negative outlook can lead to a cycle of self-pity and despair, making it difficult to find purpose in life.

Acknowledging the challenges we face and processing our emotions is important, but playing the victim prevents us from growing and learning from these experiences. We empower ourselves to make changes and create a better future by accepting responsibility for our lives. In addition, complaining about our problems affects those around us and detracts from the severity of other people's struggles. Someone will always have it worse, and it is important to keep that in perspective. By focusing on what we can control, such as our thoughts, behaviours, and reactions, we can find meaning and purpose in life, regardless of our circumstances.

ACTION STEPS:

- *Take responsibility:* The first step in avoiding a victim mindset is taking responsibility for your own life. This means acknowledging that you have the power to make choices and take action, even when things are difficult. Instead of blaming external circumstances or others for your problems, focus on what you can control and take steps to improve your situation.
- *Reframe your thinking:* Our mindset can have a powerful impact on our behaviour and emotions. To avoid a victim mindset, try reframing your thinking to focus on solutions and opportunities rather than problems and limitations. For example, instead of thinking, "I can't do this because of X," try thinking, "How can I work around X to achieve my goals?"
- *Cultivate resilience:* Resilience is the ability to bounce back from adversity and overcome challenges. To avoid a victim mindset, it's important to cultivate resilience and develop coping strategies for dealing with difficult situations. This

might include things like practising self-care, building a support system, setting achievable goals, and cultivating a positive outlook. Remember that setbacks and failures are a natural part of life, and how we respond to them ultimately determines our success.

KEEPING COMMITMENTS

Designation: Personal Responsibility, Reliability

LESSON:

Keeping your commitments is a crucial aspect of building and maintaining relationships with others. People rely on you to do what you say you will do, and when you don't follow through, it can damage their trust and perception of you. Additionally, consistently fulfilling your obligations earns you a reputation as a dependable and trustworthy individual. It is essential to be aware of the impact your actions have on others and to strive to uphold your commitments, even if it requires effort or sacrifice. Remember, people have long memories, and how you conduct yourself today will shape how you are perceived for years to come. Being mindful of your commitments and trying to follow through on them can contribute significantly to the growth of your personal and professional networks.

In addition to being reliable, taking responsibility for your actions and their outcomes is also important. If you fail to fulfill your commitments or make mistakes, own up to them and take steps to correct them. This shows integrity and a strong character and can help to build trust and respect among your colleagues and associates. Taking responsibility can also help you learn from your mistakes and avoid making similar errors in the future. By upholding your commitments and taking responsibility for your actions, you can establish a positive reputation and demonstrate your reliability and dependability to those around you.

ACTION STEPS:
- *Be intentional about what you commit to:* Before committing, take the time to evaluate whether you have the time, resources, and energy to follow through. Consider the potential impact on your other commitments, and be honest about whether you can realistically fulfill the role. By being intentional about what you commit to, you can avoid overcommitting and increase your chances of keeping your commitments.
- *Prioritize your commitments:* Once you've committed, prioritize it and ensure it's at the top of your to-do list. This may mean rearranging your schedule, delegating tasks, or saying no to other commitments. By prioritizing your commitments, you're more likely to follow through on them and fulfill your obligations.
- *Communicate openly and honestly:* If you cannot keep a commitment, communicate openly and honestly with the other party as soon as possible. Explain the situation, offer an apology if appropriate, and work together to find a solution that works for both parties. By being transparent and honest, you can maintain trust and respect in your relationships and avoid damaging your reputation.

SEEKING HELP WHEN YOU NEED IT

Designation: Personal Responsibility, Humility, Collaboration

LESSON:

It is a sign of strength and wisdom to seek help and guidance when needed. We are not meant to carry the weight of life's challenges alone, and there are resources available that can assist us in navigating difficult times. Whether seeking medical attention for health concerns, speaking with a therapist for mental health support, seeking advice from financial experts, or seeking guidance in finding employment, taking advantage of the resources available to us is an essential step in improving and enhancing our lives. Relying on the knowledge and experience of others can help us avoid making costly mistakes and speed up the process of growth and progress. Additionally, seeking support can help us build a support system and create a community that can offer us encouragement and motivation when needed. Remember, it takes courage to ask for help, but it is a crucial step in becoming the best version of yourself.

It is a common misconception that seeking help is a sign of weakness. On the contrary, it takes immense strength to acknowledge one's limitations and seek assistance in areas causing difficulty. The resources available today have never been more abundant and accessible, so there is no need to suffer in silence. Utilizing these resources can lead to a more fulfilling life and better sense of well-being.

It is important to remember that unaddressed problems often grow and become more complex. Taking advantage of available resources can help you avoid this scenario, allowing you to address problems in their earliest stages and get a handle on them. Whether through therapy, financial advice, or physical treatment, seeking help can have a profound impact on your life. Furthermore, consulting with experts in various fields can also provide valuable insights, perspectives, and solutions you might not have thought of on your own. Utilizing the knowledge and expertise of others can lead to a more well-rounded understanding of a problem and a more effective solution.

Don't be afraid to seek help when and where you need it. It can be a valuable asset to your life and a key factor in ensuring a more fulfilling and prosperous future.

ACTION STEPS:

- *Identify your needs:* Identify the areas of your life you need help with. This could be related to your mental or physical health, personal relationships, or professional development.
- *Research resources:* Research resources that are available to you. This could include therapy or counselling services, support groups, mentorship programs, or online courses. Look for resources that align with your needs and budget.
- *Reach out:* Seek help and support. This could mean making an appointment with a therapist or counsellor, joining a support group, or contacting a mentor or friend for advice. Be open and honest about your needs and goals, and ask for help when you need it.
- *Be proactive:* Finally, seek help and make changes in your life. It's important to take ownership of your journey and to be willing to work to achieve your goals. Remember that seeking help is a sign of strength and there is no shame in asking for support when needed.

GIVING PAUSE BEFORE JUDGMENT

Designation: Personal Responsibility, Emotional Intelligence, Empathy

LESSON:

Do not judge others. Everyone is guilty of it at some point, and thoughts happen whether you'd like them to or not, but do not express those thoughts outwardly. Giving pause before judgment is a crucial aspect of personal growth and success. In our fast-paced world, it's easy to form opinions quickly, but it's essential to remember that this snap judgment can often be misguided or incomplete. When we pause before judgment, we allow ourselves to step back from a situation and consider all the different perspectives and factors that may be at play. This allows us to better understand a situation and the people involved, which in turn helps us make more informed and thoughtful decisions.

Giving pause also allows us to avoid being reactive and approach situations calmly and collectedly. When we react impulsively, we risk saying or doing something we may later regret, which can damage our relationships and professional reputation. It also allows us to cultivate empathy and understanding. When we slow down and consider different perspectives, we develop a deeper understanding of the people and situations around us, which in turn helps us build stronger and more meaningful relationships. Keep in mind that everyone has their own journey and unique experiences that shape their perspectives and beliefs. When we give pause before judgment, we acknowledge and respect that diversity, which can foster a more inclusive and understanding environment.

ACTION STEPS:

- *Practise empathy:* One of the best ways to avoid judging others is to practise empathy. Put yourself in other people's shoes and try to see things from their perspective. By understanding their motivations and experiences, you'll be less likely to jump to conclusions or make assumptions about them.
- *Reframe your thinking:* When you find yourself judging someone, try to reframe your thinking. Instead of criticizing or blaming them, focus on their actions or behaviours and what you can learn from them. Ask yourself why they might have acted the way they did and how you can use that information to improve your own behaviour.
- *Look for common ground:* Finally, try to find common ground with the people you encounter. Whether working with someone on a project or just chatting with someone in line at the grocery store, look for areas of shared interest or experience. By finding common ground, you can build connections and foster understanding rather than resorting to judgment.

INTERNAL WEAK LINKS

Designation: Self-Awareness, Self-Improvement

LESSON:

Just like a team is only as much of a driving force as their weakest link, this also applies to each person independently. The analogy of a person being a product of their own internal weakest link is an excellent way to understand the relationship between our personality, strengths, and weaknesses. It reminds us that our lives are shaped by the aspects of ourselves that hold us back the most. Just like a chain is as strong as its weakest link, we are only as capable as our weakest character traits. Our personality, strengths, and weaknesses all work together to create the person we are, and it's essential to recognize the impact they have on our lives.

Our weaknesses can hold us back and prevent us from reaching our full potential. On the other hand, our strengths can give us the drive and determination to overcome those weaknesses and make significant progress in our lives. To grow and develop, it's important to identify our internal weakest links and work to strengthen them. This might mean seeking out new experiences and challenges that push us out of our comfort zones or working with a coach or therapist to address underlying issues. It's also essential to cultivate and develop our strengths; by doing so, we can turn our weaknesses into strengths and become more capable and confident individuals. This requires us to be reflective, honest, and open-minded about who we are and what we need to work on. By recognizing and working to strengthen our weaknesses and cultivate our strengths, we can overcome obstacles, reach our full potential, and live a fulfilling life.

ACTION STEPS:
- *Identify the weak links:* The first step in combating internal weak links is to identify what they are. Take some time to reflect on your behaviour, thoughts, and beliefs that may be holding you back. You can also ask for feedback from trusted friends or colleagues. Once you have identified your weak links, you can start improving them.
- *Develop a plan to improve:* Once you have identified your

weak links, you can develop a plan to improve them. This could involve setting specific goals, seeking resources or support, and practising new habits or behaviours. Make your plan realistic and achievable, and focus on one or two weak links at a time, rather than trying to tackle everything at once.

- *Hold yourself accountable:* Finally, it's important to hold yourself accountable for your progress. This means tracking your progress toward your goals, regularly checking in with yourself to see how you're doing, and being honest about where you still need to improve. You can also enlist the help of a trusted friend, coach, or mentor to help keep you accountable and provide support and encouragement along the way.

PRIDE IN YOUR APPEARANCE

Designation: Personal Responsibility, Self-Care, Perception

LESSON:

Take pride in your appearance when in or out of work, in public, and at home. When in the workplace, taking pride in your appearance demonstrates professionalism and respect for your colleagues and the company. Dressing appropriately for your job and maintaining a clean and polished appearance conveys that you take your responsibilities seriously and are committed to doing your best work.

In public, taking pride in your appearance can also reflect your values and character. It shows that you have respect for yourself and others and that you are mindful of your impact on those around you. Whether running errands, attending a social event, or simply going about your day, taking care of your appearance can help you feel more confident and in control. At home, taking pride in your appearance can also play a role in maintaining a healthy and positive living environment. When you take care of your appearance, you are more likely to take care of other aspects of your life, such as your health, hygiene, and surroundings. It can also help foster a sense of self-respect and personal responsibility, which can positively impact your overall well-being.

By maintaining a clean and polished appearance, individuals can demonstrate their professionalism, respect for themselves and others, and commitment to personal and professional growth.

ACTION STEPS:

- *Define your personal style:* Take some time to define your personal style and identify the types of clothes, hairstyles, and accessories that make you feel confident and comfortable. Look for inspiration in fashion magazines, blogs, or social media, and experiment with different styles until you find the ones that best reflect your personality and preferences.
- *Practise good grooming habits:* Maintaining good grooming habits is an essential part of taking pride in your appearance. This might include bathing regularly, keeping your hair and nails neat and tidy, and taking care of your skin. You might also consider investing in quality skin-care products, cosmetics, or grooming tools to help you look and feel your best.
- *Pay attention to details:* Finally, the details can make a big difference in your overall appearance. This might include

accessorizing with jewellery or scarves, choosing clothes that flatter your body type, and making sure your clothes are clean and wrinkle-free. Focusing on these small details can help you feel more put together and confident in your appearance.

ACT IN PRIVATE AS YOU DO IN PUBLIC

Designation: Personal Responsibility, Integrity, Authenticity

LESSON:

Adopting a consistent demeanour, whether in private or public, is a sign of maturity and professionalism. It shows that you are in control of your emotions and actions and that you respect those around you. When you behave in a certain way in private and then switch to a completely different behaviour in public, it can be confusing and even off-putting to others. People expect consistency from those they interact with, and acting differently in private and public can erode that trust. You can prevent embarrassing situations or unwanted words from slipping out when you act in private as you do in public. When we are relaxed and in the comfort of our own space, it can be easy to let our guard down and say things we might not normally say. By maintaining a professional demeanour, even in private, you can ensure that you never say anything that could be damaging to your reputation.

This trait is a hallmark of self-discipline and self-respect. It helps build trust with others and prevents unwanted situations from occurring. It is a simple yet powerful way to demonstrate professionalism and respect for those around you.

ACTION STEPS:

- *Develop strong personal values:* Personal values are principles that guide your behaviour and decision-making. Developing strong personal values that align with your public actions can help you act consistently in private. Reflect on what you stand for and what is important to you, and use these values as a guide for your private actions.
- *Hold yourself accountable:* Holding yourself accountable for your actions, both in public and in private, can help you act with integrity and consistency. Be honest with yourself about your behaviour and strive to act in alignment with your personal values at all times.
- *Practise mindfulness:* Mindfulness is being present and fully engaged in the current moment. By practising mindfulness, you can become more aware of your thoughts and behaviours and make conscious choices about how you act in private. Take time to reflect on your behaviour, thoughts, and feelings, and use this awareness to align your private actions with your public persona.

AWARENESS OF ADVICE SOURCES

Designation: Personal Responsibility, Importance of Selection

LESSON:

It is important to be discerning when seeking advice and guidance from various sources. While it may be tempting to follow the advice of someone who appears to have all the answers, it is crucial to remember that not all sources are created equal. Some "gurus" or "life coaches" may simply be playing to a particular audience, using buzzwords and catchphrases to capture attention, without offering substantive solutions to life's problems. These individuals may be well-versed in public speaking, but their words are often empty and lacking in real-world application. It is up to you to determine the credibility of a source and to carefully evaluate the advice being offered. Just because someone appears confident and articulate, it doesn't necessarily mean they have the answers to the problems you are facing.

It is essential to remember that true success and growth come from hard work and dedication, not just from hearing motivational words. The real answers lie within you, and only through introspection, self-reflection, and persistent effort will you find the solutions you seek. The journey to self-discovery and success is personal, requiring a great deal of effort and determination. Don't be misled by those who offer easy solutions and quick fixes—the path to success is never a straight line, but with persistence and hard work, you can achieve your goals and live a fulfilling life.

Remember that success doesn't come from following what others tell you or listening to their "woke" messages. True success and growth come from taking personal responsibility and putting in the effort to make a real difference in your life. Rather than relying on temporary motivators or easy fixes, embracing the grind and the struggle is crucial. This means putting in the hard work, day in and day out, to achieve your goals. Whether through training, learning, or other means, the key to success is taking ownership of your growth and never being satisfied with mediocrity. Don't be misled by false gurus and their empty promises, but instead, forge your own path and make the most of your potential.

ACTION STEPS:

- *Seek out diverse perspectives:* It's important to seek out various perspectives and sources of advice when making decisions or seeking guidance. This might involve asking for feedback from friends, family members, colleagues, or experts in your field. Be open to considering different points of view and incorporating multiple perspectives into your decision-making process.
- *Evaluate the source of advice:* When considering advice from various sources, it's important to evaluate the source's credibility. Be mindful of biases or conflicts of interest that may influence the advice. Consider the experience, knowledge, and expertise of the person giving the advice and whether they have a track record of success in the area you seek advice on.
- *Trust your own judgment:* While seeking advice from others is important, ultimately, it's up to you to make the final decision. Trust your judgment and instincts, and be willing to take risks and make mistakes. Recognize that you are the expert on your own life and goals, and use the advice of others as a tool to help you make informed decisions, but not as the sole determinant of your choices.

SEEKING FEEDBACK AND CRITICISM

Designation: Growth Mindset, Open-Mindedness

LESSON:

It's important to understand that seeking feedback and criticism is a crucial aspect of personal growth and development. Whether it's from your coworkers, colleagues, superiors, or mentors, it's essential to actively seek the truth about your strengths and weaknesses. This will help you to see yourself objectively, identify areas for improvement, and work toward becoming the best version of yourself. However, it's important to approach this process with an open mind and a willingness to learn. You may not always like what you hear, but if the feedback is constructive and well-intentioned, it can be extremely valuable in helping you grow and evolve. If a particular critique is brought up multiple times, it's important to take it seriously and consider making changes.

To get the most out of this process, it's important to approach the feedback with a positive attitude and to be open to making changes. Ask specific questions to better understand the areas where you need to improve and seek advice and guidance from those giving you the feedback. They may have valuable insights and suggestions to help you make the necessary changes. Overall, seeking feedback from those around you is a great way to gain new perspectives, learn from others, and improve yourself personally and professionally.

ACTION STEPS:

- *Be open to feedback:* It's important to approach feedback with an open mind and a willingness to learn. Avoid getting defensive or dismissive when someone offers criticism, even if it's not what you want to hear. Instead, listen carefully to the feedback and take it as an opportunity to grow and improve.
- *Ask specific questions:* When seeking feedback, asking specific questions about areas where you want to improve can be helpful. For example, you might ask for feedback on a particular project, a specific aspect of your work, or your

communication skills. By asking specific questions, you can focus on the feedback and get more targeted insights that can help you improve.
- *Use the feedback constructively:* Once you've received feedback, use it constructively to make changes and improvements. This might mean developing a plan to address areas of weakness, seeking additional resources or training, or simply being more mindful of your behaviour in the future. By using the feedback constructively, you can demonstrate your willingness to learn and improve and build a reputation as someone who takes feedback seriously.

LIVING WITHIN YOUR MEANS

Designation: Financial Responsibility, Personal Finance

LESSON:

Living within your means involves avoiding excessive debt, understanding the difference between wants and needs, and making responsible choices regarding spending. This can help you build a strong financial foundation, providing stability in your life and reducing stress. Ultimately, it's important to understand that financial success is not a one-time event but a journey that requires consistent effort and focus. By making responsible financial decisions, seeking opportunities to increase your income, and living within your means, you can create a brighter financial future for yourself and your loved ones.

Moreover, it's important to understand the power of positive thinking regarding finances. What we believe about money and our ability to earn it can greatly impact our financial success.

By shifting our mindset to one of abundance and possibility, we open ourselves up to new opportunities and attract more prosperity. This doesn't mean simply visualizing large sums of money coming in—it requires taking action and developing the skills necessary to earn what we desire. Whether expanding your education, networking, or finding new ways to bring value to others, the key is to take control of your financial future and not to simply rely on luck or chance. Additionally, it's crucial to have a financial plan and to stick to it. This means creating a budget, setting financial goals, and tracking your spending. By having a clear picture of your income and expenses, you can make informed decisions about allocating your resources and working toward a more secure financial future. Remember, financial success is not about living a life of deprivation—it's about making smart choices and being disciplined to stick to a plan. With the right mindset, strategies, and habits, you can achieve financial freedom and live the life you truly desire.

> **Note:** In today's economy, it can be difficult to set a pace financially and still make time to enjoy yourself. You may be working two or even three jobs to get by, pay for school, or support whatever other financial drains you have. It's important to seek opportunities and move up where possible to ensure your hard work is recognized.
>
> It is also important to understand that how you handle your finances reflects your overall life-management skills. Setting clear financial goals and making smart decisions in regard to spending and saving can give you peace of mind and a sense of control over your life. Remember that building wealth takes time and consistency, and it requires you to make smart financial decisions continually.

ACTION STEPS:

- *Create a budget:* Create a budget and track your spending. This will help you to understand your income and expenses and identify areas where you can cut back. Be sure to include all expenses, including bills, groceries, transportation, and entertainment.
- *Prioritize your spending:* Prioritize your spending and focus on the essentials. This may mean cutting back on discretionary expenses like dining out or entertainment to ensure you can afford the necessities. Make sure to save a portion of your monthly income, even if it's just a small amount.
- *Avoid debt:* Avoid taking on debt whenever possible. Credit card debt, in particular, can quickly accumulate and become difficult to pay off. If you need to take on debt, try to pay it off as quickly as possible to minimize interest charges.
- *Plan ahead:* Plan ahead and save for unanticipated future expenses, such as car repairs or medical bills. By setting aside money each month for these expenses, you can avoid financial stress and be better prepared when unexpected expenses arise.
- *Shop smart:* Look for deals and discounts whenever possible. This could include buying in bulk, shopping at discount stores, or using coupons or promo codes. By being mindful of your spending and looking for ways to save, you can stretch your budget further and live within your means.

LEAVE PLACES IN EQUAL OR BETTER CONDITION THAN YOU FOUND THEM

Designation: Responsibility, Stewardship

LESSON:

Leave places in equal or better condition than you found them. This act is an important aspect of responsible and ethical behaviour. It reflects an individual's respect for their surroundings and those who will occupy it after leaving. The principle applies to various environments, from a shared office space to a public park. By ensuring that the spaces you occupy are tidy and well-maintained, you demonstrate your own level of discipline and care and contribute to the community's overall well-being.

In today's fast-paced world, it is easy to forget about the small details that make a big difference in our surroundings. However, by cleaning up after ourselves, we can create a more positive and productive environment for everyone. This includes being mindful of the impact our actions have on the natural environment. By not littering, we can help preserve the beauty and integrity of our planet. This behaviour is not just a matter of manners, but also a reflection of our values and how we perceive the world. By committing to leaving places in better condition than we found them, we can set a positive example for those around us and make a tangible difference in our communities and the environment.

ACTION STEPS:
- *Practise awareness:* Practise awareness of your surroundings and the impact of your actions. Be mindful of how you are using the space and the resources available. Take note

of any damage or areas needing improvement, and try to address them.
- *Bring what you need:* Bring what you need to take care of the space, such as garbage bags, cleaning supplies, or gardening tools. Use these resources to pick up litter, clean up spills, or tend to any plants or green spaces. You can be proactive in maintaining the space by bringing what you need.
- *Lead by example:* Lead by example and encourage others to do the same. If you see someone littering or damaging the space, kindly remind them of the importance of caring for the area. You can create a culture of respect and responsibility for the environment by setting an example for others.
- *Get involved:* Consider getting involved in local cleanup efforts or volunteering with organizations that work to improve public spaces. This can be a great way to contribute to your community and make a positive impact on the environment.
- *Spread the word:* Finally, spread the word and encourage others to care for public spaces. Share your experiences and the importance of taking responsibility for our environment. By raising awareness and educating others, you can help to create a positive change in our communities.

IMPACT OF DECISIONS—PAST, PRESENT, FUTURE

Designation: Personal Responsibility, Consequence Awareness

LESSON:

It's essential to recognize that the choices we make today can have consequences in the future. Whether in our personal lives, careers, or relationships, our actions have a ripple effect that can impact us and those around us for years to come. At the same time, it's important to understand that our past actions also have positive and negative consequences. The choices we've made and the paths we've taken have shaped who we are today and set us on a certain course.

It is imperative to understand that every action we take creates a chain reaction of consequences, both positive and negative. Our past actions have brought us to where we are today and shaped our future, and the choices we make now will shape our tomorrow. As such, it's crucial to be mindful of our actions and their impact. Every decision we make should be taken with care and consideration for the long-term consequences.

In our careers, for example, the choices we make can have a significant impact on our future success. Whether it's taking on a new project, accepting a new job offer, or investing in new skills and training, it's important to weigh the potential consequences and make informed decisions to help us achieve our goals. The same is true in our personal lives. The decisions we make, whether related to our relationships, health, or financial stability, have the power to shape our future and determine the course of our lives. By making informed decisions and taking control of our future, we can create a path toward a better tomorrow.

ACTION STEPS:
- *Reflect on past decisions:* Take the time to reflect on past decisions and the resulting consequences. Think about what worked well and what didn't, and consider how your decisions affected yourself and others. Reflecting on past decisions can help you learn from your mistakes and avoid making similar errors in the future.

- *Consider the present consequences:* When making a decision, it's important to consider the consequences in the present. Consider how your decision will impact yourself and others in the immediate future, and weigh the pros and cons. Consider the potential risks and benefits of different options, and choose the option that best aligns with your values and goals.
- *Anticipate future consequences:* It's important to also consider the long-term consequences of your decisions. Think about how your decision will impact yourself and others in the future, and consider any unintended consequences that may arise. Consider the potential ripple effects of your decision and how it might impact your future goals and plans. By anticipating future consequences, you can make more informed decisions that align with your values and goals in the long term.

DECISIONS WE MAKE

Designation: Decision-Making, Self-Awareness

LESSON:

Making decisions is a central aspect of life, shaping our character and ultimately our destiny. Whether we choose to do good or bad, the outcome of these decisions will determine the quality of our life experiences. It is important to be mindful of our choices and to strive to make good decisions that will bring us closer to our goals and aspirations. This can be a challenging task, but it is essential to achieve greatness and success.

One of the keys to making good decisions is to learn from our experiences. If we make a good choice, it is important to reflect on why it was a good decision and how we can replicate it. This can involve taking mental notes or even writing down our observations. By doing this, we can create a formula for success to refer to when making future decisions. In the same vein, if we make a bad decision or have a negative experience, it is equally important to learn from it. We can do this by examining what went wrong and why it didn't work out. This will help us to avoid making the same mistakes in the future and instead make better choices that will lead to a more successful outcome.

Ultimately, life is about growth and progress. By constantly striving to make better decisions and learn from our experiences, we can continue to improve and achieve our goals. Whether faced with good or bad days, the key is to keep pushing forward and never give up on our dreams. By staying focused and driven, we can overcome any obstacle and attain our desired success.

ACTION STEPS:

- *Gather information:* Gather as much information as possible before making any decisions. This could involve conducting research, seeking advice from experts, or collecting data from various sources. The more information you have, the better equipped you will be to make an informed decision.
- *Consider alternatives:* When making decisions, it's important to consider various alternatives. Don't simply choose the first option that comes to mind—take the time to weigh the pros and cons of different alternatives and consider the potential outcomes of each.
- *Use a structured decision-making process:* A structured decision-making process can help you make more effective decisions. One common approach is to identify the problem

or decision, gather relevant information, identify alternatives, evaluate the alternatives, and choose the best option. By using a structured process, you can ensure that you are considering all relevant factors and making a decision based on a thorough analysis of the situation. Additionally, if the decision doesn't go as planned, it is important to review the decision-making process and see how you can improve for the next time.

ALIGNING STRENGTHS WITH GOALS

Designation: Utilizing Strengths, Forward Thinking

LESSON:

If your goals aren't aligned with your strengths, make your strengths line up with your goals. One of the most important things to understand in life is that everyone has unique strengths and weaknesses. Therefore, it's essential to be self-aware and understand your strengths. If your goals don't align with your strengths, achieving those goals can be incredibly difficult. That's why it's so important to ensure your strengths align with your goals. This doesn't mean you shouldn't challenge yourself and try to develop new skills; rather, you should use your strengths as a foundation and build upon them to achieve your goals.

One effective way to do this is to identify your top strengths and use them as a starting point for goal setting. For example, if one of your strengths is excellent interpersonal skills, you may want to focus on building a career in a field where those skills are in high demand, such as sales, marketing, or customer service. On the other hand, if your strength lies in data analysis, you may want to focus on a career in finance, engineering, or research.

You'll be setting yourself up for success by aligning your strengths with your goals. This is because you'll be putting your strengths to work and leveraging them to reach your goals. Additionally, you'll also be doing what you love, which will increase your motivation and help you to stay committed to your goals over the long term.

ACTION STEPS:

- *Identify your strengths:* Start by identifying your strengths. What are you good at? What comes naturally to you? This could be a particular skillset, personality trait, or area of expertise. Make a list of your strengths and reflect on how you have used them in the past.
- *Reassess your goals:* Look at your goals and reassess whether they align with your strengths. If they don't, consider how you can adjust your goals to leverage your strengths better. For example, if your goal is to become a successful writer, but your strength is public speaking, consider how you can incorporate public speaking into your writing career by doing book tours or speaking engagements.
- *Develop your strengths:* Once you have identified and reassessed your strengths, focus on developing your strengths to better align with your goals. This could involve taking classes, finding a mentor, or practising your skills regularly. By improving your strengths, you can increase your confidence and effectiveness in pursuing your goals.
- *Be flexible:* It's important to be flexible and adaptable as you work toward aligning your strengths with your goals. You may need to adjust your goals or your approach as you

gain new insights and experiences. Remember that it's okay to make mistakes and change direction if necessary. The most important thing is to stay focused on developing your strengths and aligning them with your goals.

LIFE IS WHAT YOU MAKE IT

Designation: Personal Responsibility

LESSON:

"Life is what you make it" may sound like a simple and superficial saying, but it actually contains a deep truth that is often overlooked. At its core, this saying is an acknowledgement that we are the architects of our own lives, and that our choices and actions profoundly impact the quality and direction of our experiences. It is easy to fall into the trap of conformity, where we follow the expectations and norms of our society without much thought or reflection. This can be a comfortable and safe way to live, but it can also lead to a sense of emptiness and dissatisfaction as we fail to explore the full range of our own desires and aspirations.

The truth is we have tremendous freedom and agency in our lives. We can choose to pursue our passions and interests, seek out new experiences and challenges, and push the boundaries of what we believe is possible. We can talk to anyone we want to talk to, go anywhere we want to go, and do most things we want to do—as long as we are willing to take responsibility for our choices and actions. This requires us to step outside our comfort zones and challenge the limiting beliefs and assumptions that hold us back. We must be willing to embrace uncertainty and risk and trust in our abilities and potential. This can be a difficult and intimidating process, but it is also incredibly liberating and rewarding.

We have the power to shape our destinies and explore the full range of our own desires and aspirations. This requires us to step outside the cage of conformity and embrace our freedom and agency. By doing so, we can unlock the full potential of our lives and create a future that is truly our own.

ACTION STEPS:

- *Set goals:* One way to take control of your life is to set goals that are important to you. These goals can be short term or long term and can relate to different areas of your life, such as career, relationships, health, or personal growth. By setting goals and working toward them, you can give your life direction and purpose.
- *Take action:* Once you have set your goals, it's important to take action toward achieving them. This may involve breaking your goals into smaller, manageable steps and then taking consistent action toward completing those steps. Taking action, even if it's small, can help you build momentum and move closer to achieving your goals.
- *Cultivate a positive mindset:* Your mindset can greatly impact your life. By cultivating a positive mindset, you can approach challenges with optimism and resilience and see setbacks as opportunities for growth. You can cultivate a positive mindset by focusing on what you are grateful for, practising self-compassion, and surrounding yourself with positive and supportive people.

You could read one thousand quotes or one thousand books, but if they don't mean anything to you, you likely won't remember them. Quality is better than quantity.

VII.

CONCLUSION

And in the end, the key to success lies in having a clear vision of what you want, and a willingness to do whatever it takes to achieve it.

AS THIS BOOK COMES TO A CLOSE, I WANT TO EMPHASIZE that the lessons, considerations, and advice I've shared are not just theoretical concepts but practical wisdom I've gained through years of blood, sweat, and tears. They've been tested and redefined and stood the test of time. In these pages, I have shared my hard-earned insights and practical wisdom on various aspects of life. Drawing from my own experiences and observations, I have sought to empower you with actionable tools, inspire your personal growth, and contribute to your success in different domains. I'm grateful for the opportunity to share these insights with you and provide valuable guidance as you navigate the complexities of life, and I hope they've resonated with you. But remember, this journey of self-improvement is not a one-time event. It is a continuous process that demands effort, discipline, and resilience. It's about embracing challenges, learning from failures, and never settling for anything less than excellence. Embrace challenges, learn from failures, and keep pushing forward with a relentless pursuit of excellence. I believe that by embodying the principles discussed in this book, you can overcome any obstacle and achieve greatness in all aspects of your life.

Be sure to keep in mind the repetition of many of the action steps for multiple lessons. That is no coincidence. It might've even become tedious to read them repeatedly, and you may have said to yourself, "Okay, I get it," which is great. This is because so many things in life come down to concepts like breaking things into smaller, more manageable steps, setting clear and achievable goals, practising mindfulness, developing a growth mindset, practising gratitude, etc. You need to practise those things often for a journey of less resistance.

One of the most powerful ways to grow and develop as a person is to observe and learn from others. By watching the actions and words of those around us, we can gain insights into how our own behaviours and attitudes might affect the people in our lives. This kind of learning requires a certain level of humility and self-awareness, as we must be willing to acknowledge our own limitations and learn from the wisdom and experience of others. If we approach this kind of learning with a genuine desire to understand and connect with others, we can gain a wealth of useful information and insights. There are lessons to be learned at all stages of life, and by embracing and analyzing these lessons, we can become better equipped to navigate the challenges and opportunities that come our way. It is a large responsibility to take on the role of bettering yourself, but it is easier than you might think. By cultivating a curious and open-minded approach to life, we can gain a deep understanding of ourselves and others and use that knowledge to build strong and meaningful relationships.

I hope you act on the actionable steps provided, using them as a roadmap to achieve your personal and professional success. Stay focused on your goals, stay disciplined in your approach, stay resilient in the face of challenges, and never stop learning. Success may not come easy, but with unwavering commitment, continuous learning, and a relentless pursuit of excellence, you can achieve greatness. As you continue on your journey of self-improvement, remember the foundational importance of discipline and resilience, the significance of productivity and personal responsibility, the value of teamwork and relationships, and the need for constant personal development. Embrace these principles and keep pushing forward, adapting to changing circumstances, expanding your horizons, and investing in your growth, well-being, and self-awareness.

If you want to succeed in any aspect of your life, it all comes down to your level of commitment and effort. No matter what your goal may be, taking even the smallest steps toward it every day can help you make progress over time. Whether striving for career success, stronger relationships, or personal growth, you need to maintain a balance in all areas of your life. Different areas may require more attention at different times, but neglecting any key area can throw off the balance you've worked hard to achieve, potentially affecting other areas of your life. So, commit to putting in the work and maintaining that balance, and success will follow.

I hope you found this book both informative and motivating, that it helps you on your journey toward self-improvement, and that you enjoyed reading it as much as I enjoyed writing it. I cannot guarantee that the most difficult parts of your life are over when reading this. Considering all that is written here and what you know to be the right path, coupled with the help of a growth mindset and a hunger for knowledge and personal development, I have no doubt in my mind that you have what it takes when it comes to life.

Your journey continues.

ACKNOWLEDGEMENTS

There is less strength in solitude.

- My good friend *Kaity Baker* for her many hours spent as my adviser and "sounding board" in the later stages of this book to help me organize my chaotic groups of ideas; and her mother, *Donna*, for helping her to become the kind, supportive, and selfless person she is today. Stay positive. Stay motivated. Continue dreaming and setting goals for yourself.
- Another friend, but a little further away, *Melanie Brown*, for your patience, suggestions, and putting up with my roller coaster of thoughts and ideas. You're more patient than you realize.

- The *Scribe Media* team for their time, assistance, skills, knowledge, and expertise in book development and publishing. The ongoing transparency of their process and support transformed my idea into the book we see today. An amazing team to work with.

REFERENCES

LOCARD'S EXCHANGE PRINCIPLE:

Crime Investigation: Physical Evidence and the Police Laboratory. New York: Interscience Publishers, Inc., 1953. Paul L. Kirk.

NEWTON'S FIRST LAW:

Newton's Laws—Lesson 1—Newton's First Law of Motion. *The Physics Classroom.*

www.ingramcontent.com/pod-product-compliance
Lightning Source LLC
Chambersburg PA
CBHW030442090526
44586CB00044B/517